THE UNFINISHED AGENDA:

A NEW VISION FOR CHILD DEVELOPMENT AND EDUCATION

A Statement by the Research and Policy Committee of the Committee for Economic Development

CED

Library of Congress Cataloging-in-Publication Data

The Unfinished Agenda: A New Vision for Child Development and
Education.
p. cm.
"A Statement by the Research and Policy Committee for the
Committee for Economic Development."
Includes bibliographical references.
ISBN 0-87186-793-1 : (library binding) : $15.00. --
ISBN 0-87186-093-7 : (paperback) : $12.50
1. Education--Social aspects--United States. 2. Child development--
United States. 3. Education--United States--Aims and objectives.
4. Educational change--United States. 5. Education and state--
United States.
I. Committee for Economic Development.
II. Committee for Economic Development. Research and Policy
Committee.
LC191.4.U54 1991
370. 19' 0973--dc20

First printing in bound-book form: 1991
Paperback: $12.50
Library binding: $15.00
Printed in the United States of America
Design: Rowe & Ballantine

COMMITTEE FOR ECONOMIC DEVELOPMENT
477 Madison Avenue, New York, N.Y. 10022
(212) 688-2063

1700 K Street, N.W., Washington, D.C. 20006
(202) 296-5860

CONTENTS

iv

THE UNFINISHED AGENDA:

A NEW VISION FOR CHILD DEVELOPMENT AND EDUCATION

RESPONSIBILITY FOR CED STATEMENTS ON NATIONAL POLICY

The Committee for Economic Development is an independent research and educational organization of some 250 business leaders and educators. CED is nonprofit, nonpartisan and nonpolitical. Its purpose is to propose policies that bring about steady economic growth at high employment and reasonably stable prices, increased productivity and living standards, greater and more equal opportunity for every citizen, and improved quality of life for all.

All CED policy recommendations must have the approval of trustees on the Research and Policy Committee. This committee is directed under the bylaws which emphasize that "all research is to be thoroughly objective in character, and the approach in each instance is to be from the standpoint of the general welfare and not from that of any special political or economic group." The committee is aided by a Research Advisory Board of leading social scientists and by a small permanent professional staff.

The Research and Policy Committee does not attempt to pass judgment on any pending specific legislative proposals; its purpose is to urge careful consideration of the objectives set forth in this statement and of the best means of accomplishing those objectives.

Each statement is preceded by extensive discussions, meetings, and exchange of memoranda. The research is undertaken by a subcommittee, assisted by advisors chosen for their competence in the field under study.

The full Research and Policy Committee participates in the drafting of recommendations. Likewise, the trustees on the drafting subcommittee vote to approve or disapprove a policy statement, and they share with the Research and Policy Committee the privilege of submitting individual comments for publication.

Except for the members of the Research and Policy Committee and the responsible subcommittee, the recommendations presented herein are not necessarily endorsed by other trustees or by the advisors, contributors, staff members, or others associated with CED.

RESEARCH AND POLICY COMMITTEE

ADVISORS

WILLIAM ARAMONY
National Chairman
United Way of America

T. BERRY BRAZELTON
Professor of Pediatrics
Harvard Medical School

JOSEPH FERNANDEZ
Chancellor
New York City Public Schools

CAROLYN GASTON
Student Success Advocate
Albuquerque Public Schools

RAE GRAD
Executive Director
National Commission to Prevent
    Infant Mortality

TOM GUSTAFSON
Speaker of the House
Florida Legislature

HENRY LEVIN
Professor of Education and
    Economics
Stanford University

MARSHA LEVINE
Associate Director
    of Education Issues
American Federation of Teachers

ARTURO MADRID
President
Tomas Rivera Center

PETER McWALTERS
Superintendent of Schools
Rochester Public Schools

JOHN OGBU
Minority Education Project
Survey Research Center
University of California
    at Berkeley

TERRY K. PETERSON
Executive Director
South Carolina EIA Joint
    Business-Education Committee

RUTH RANDALL
Professor, Education
    Administration
University of Nebraska

JERRY ROSOW
President
Work in America Institute

LISBETH SCHORR
Lecturer in Social Medicine
Harvard Medical School

ALBERT SHANKER
President
American Federation of Teachers

* LEONARD SILK
Economics Columnist
The New York Times

JULE SUGERMAN
Executive Director
Special Olympics International

P. MICHAEL TIMPANE
President
Teachers College
Columbia University

*member, Research Advisory Board.

PROJECT DIRECTOR

SANDRA KESSLER HAMBURG
Director of Education Studies
CED, New York

PROJECT COUNSELORS

SCOTT FOSLER
Vice President and Director of
    Government Studies
CED, Washington

NATHANIEL M. SEMPLE
Vice President, Secretary of
    the Research and Policy
    Committee, and Director of
    Government Relations
CED, Washington

PROJECT STAFF

TAMARA L. BERKOWER
Research Assistant

JEREMY A. LEONARD
Policy Analyst

PURPOSE OF THIS STATEMENT

As the drive to improve the public schools approaches nearly a decade of debate and experimentation, experience with reform demonstrates that the schools themselves cannot make all the changes necessary to ensure that all children will become sufficiently educated. Profound social change, particularly the dramatic increase in single-parent families, has resulted in more and more children being born at risk of failure.

The Unfinished Agenda: A New Vision for Child Development and Education represents a major step in the evolution of CED's thinking on the subject of education. The business leaders and educators on CED's board of trustees have spent close to nine years developing strategies for improving the educational achievement of all children, particularly the disadvantaged.

The first product of this effort, *Investing in Our Children: Business and the Public Schools,* issued in 1985, identified quality education as the most important economic commitment the nation could make in its future productivity and competitiveness. This report was the first issued by a business organization to target preschool education for poor children as a superior investment and one of the most effective dropout prevention measures available. In 1987, CED issued the landmark report *Children in Need: Investment Strategies for the Educationally Disadvantaged,* which addressed the needs of children at risk for failure, whose problems were largely being bypassed by early state and local education reforms. *Children in Need* outlined an effective three-part strategy for breaking the cycle of failure that included early intervention, restructuring of the schools, and programs targeted to adolescents at risk of dropping out and those who have already left the system.

A NEW STRATEGY FOR HUMAN INVESTMENT

The Unfinished Agenda goes several steps further. Its analysis of the results of the early education reform movement indicates that most state and local initiatives have been piecemeal, conflicting, and have lacked a true understanding of the complex needs that affect children's ability to learn. The report urges the nation to develop a comprehensive and coordinated strategy of human investment, one that redefines education as a process that begins at birth and encompasses all aspects of children's early development, including their physical, social, emotional and cognitive growth. The report emphasizes that the first actions we must take are to strengthen families and increase the abilities of parents to act as their children's first and most important teacher.

The report also recognizes that as we begin to prepare children better for formal schooling, we will be in danger of squandering our early investment unless we also restructure the schools to enable them to meet the diverse learning needs of their students at every stage of the educational process.

THE IMPACT OF BUSINESS

Throughout its work on improving educational achievement, CED has consistently urged business involvement in this effort. To provide data on the contributions of business, CED commissioned new research. The resulting study, titled *Business Impact on Education and Child Development Reform*, by P. Michael Timpane, president of Teachers College, Columbia University, and Laurie Miller McNeill, clearly demonstrates that the advocacy of the corporate community nationwide has been instrumental in driving the evolving agenda on reforming our system of education and child development.

For its analysis of the implications of demographic change on human resource development, *The Unfinished Agenda* also draws on illuminating research conducted for CED's recent policy report *An America That Works: A Life Cycle Approach to a Competitive Work Force* (1990). The underlying message of this report is that the profound changes in our society and economy over the past twenty years will overwhelm us unless we are willing to transform our system of human investment to ensure that every child is prepared to be a productive citizen.

ACKNOWLEDGMENTS

On behalf of the Research and Policy Committee, I would like to express our deepest appreciation to James J. Renier, chairman and chief executive officer of Honeywell, Inc., for the energy, wisdom, and commitment he demonstrated as chairman of the CED Subcommittee on Education and Child Development. Jim Renier also brought an unusually high degree of practical experience to the subcommittee process, as exemplified by his leadership of the innovative Minneapolis Success by 6 project and his work on behalf of education with the Minnesota Business Partnership and the national Business Roundtable.

We are also grateful to the outstanding group of business leaders, educators, and child care specialists, listed on pages viii and ix, who were so willing to share their time, knowledge, and expertise, which contributed so importantly to the strength of the report. Special thanks are due project director Sandra Kessler Hamburg for her leadership of a research effort that uncovered dozens of examples of innovation and success and her ability to analyze and synthesize a complex web of issues and express them in clear and compelling language.

No discussion of CED's work in education would be complete without grateful mention of CED's chairman, Owen B. Butler, retired chairman of The Procter & Gamble Company, who served as chairman of the subcommittees that produced both *Investing in Our Children* and *Children in Need*. Brad Butler's unparalleled efforts on behalf of children and education have made him one of the nation's most respected business leaders on these issues, moving *Fortune* magazine to name him "the dean of education reform."

Finally, I would like to acknowledge the important financial and intellectual contributions made by the many private and corporate foundations, listed on page 95, that have so generously supported the CED program in education and child development.

Dean P. Phypers
Chairman
Research and Policy Committee

Chapter 1

A NEW HUMAN INVESTMENT STRATEGY

After nearly a decade of debate on education reform, far too many American children continue to grow up without the fundamental skills and knowledge needed to be productive in the workplace and informed in the voting booth. The reason is clear: Our society has undergone profound economic and demographic transformations, but the social and educational institutions that prepare children to become capable and responsible adults have failed to keep pace. Unless we act swiftly and decisively to improve the way we invest in our most important resource – our nation's children – we are jeopardizing America's survival as a free and prosperous society and condemning much of a new generation to lives of poverty and despair.

In the past, society's responsibility for providing educational opportunities for children started with their entry into school. But a new understanding of how children learn makes it clear that the nation can no longer afford to wait that long. The development and education of all our children from the earliest stages of their lives must be made a national priority, and throughout that process, the needs of the whole child, from conception through adolescence, must be addressed. Children must be better prepared for school and motivated to take advantage of educational opportunities. At the same time, the nation's schools must be restructured so that they respond more effectively to the changing developmental and educational needs of children.

Our challenge is to translate this knowledge into wide-ranging action. This will require the leadership of a broad coalition from business, government, education, and the community, including parents, and the will to remove barriers and encourage cooperation and collaboration among a multitude of public- and private-sector agencies and institutions.

Some states, local communities, and schools are making important strides in linking child development with education and improving the achievement of students, but the examples of success are few and far between. Far more needs to be done, and it needs to be done quickly if we are to ensure that America remains a land of opportunity – for all our children.

*   *   *

The warning signs are clear and compelling. More children are being born into poverty and into single-parent families than ever before. Between 1970 and 1987, the poverty rate for children increased nearly 33 percent. In 1989, close to 25 percent of children under the age of six lived in poverty, and one-fourth of all births were to unmarried women. When multiple risk factors, such as poverty, family structure, and race are taken into account, as many as 40 percent of all children may be considered disadvantaged.[1]

Educationally, the United States remains a nation at risk. More than 25 percent of all students fail to graduate from high school each year, and in many major cities, half of all poor and minority students routinely drop out of school with poor skills, few job prospects, and limited opportunities in life. The outlook is not much better for many who make it to graduation. The National Assessment of Educational Progress (NAEP) reports that fewer than half of all seventeen-year-olds who are in school develop reading, writing, mathematics, or problem-solving skills adequate for success in business, government, or higher education. Although minority students have begun to narrow the achievement gap in reading and math, they still lag behind their white counterparts by about four years. Worse still for the nation's ability to compete in the global market, American students continue to rank behind many, if not most, of our major international economic competitors on almost every measure of achievement, especially in math and science.

Neither our economy nor our society can afford to lose the talents of so many of our young people. In an earlier industrial era, the economy did not need to ensure that every child was well educated, partly because the available labor pool was large enough and partly because unskilled manual labor and low-skilled manufacturing jobs were sufficiently plentiful and well-paid to absorb those without higher-level skills. This is no longer the case. In twenty years, just as the baby boom generation begins to retire, the nation could face a labor shortage severe enough to stifle business at every level. Labor force growth, which averaged 2.9 percent per year in the 1970s, will average only 1 percent in the 1990s and could actually decline in the beginning of the next century. At the same time, there will be fewer working-age people to support the burgeoning retired population, straining public and private retirement systems.[2]

Despite these troubling statistics, there are signs of hope. A new research study commissioned by CED on the impact of business involvement in education reform indicates that many states and local communities are making progress in addressing the complex web of problems that have caused the nation's educational decline.[3] Two interrelated developments are helping to shape the future direction of educational change.

First, policy makers are beginning to appreciate the true depth of the problems facing education. After watching incremental remedies fail to improve achievement and in some cases even increase the dropout rate, leaders in business, government, and education are beginning to act on the knowledge that the schools will continue to fail unless they are fundamentally restructured to make them more responsive and efficient in meeting both the academic and social needs of children and more accountable for what students actually learn.

Second, many policy leaders have begun to subscribe to a broader view of human resource development. They are starting to view early childhood development, education, social services, job training, and economic development as parts of an interdependent system of human investments, rather than as independent enterprises.

Although these trends are promising, they are still very new. They are not yet driving the education reform movement in most states and communities. Schools are still generally regarded as purely academic institutions, with little or no public recognition of the broader social mission they are undertaking.

THE UNFINISHED AGENDA

In both policy and practice, the United States is far from ensuring that all its children are prepared to succeed in a more complex and competitive world. The task of completing this unfinished agenda is enormous, but nothing less than the nation's future is at stake.

When faced with deeply ingrained societal problems, there is a tendency to look for quick and easy solutions. For example, a recent proposal in support of school choice recommends abandoning the existing public school system and leaving most educational decisions to the free market.[4] Although allowing parents greater choice of public schools can provide an important incentive for improving the quality of education, we do not believe that choice by itself will result in quality schools for all children. Relying on such single strategies tends to obscure the complexity of both the problems and the potential solutions. We do support some measures to encourage choice among public schools as part of a broader restructuring strategy. We also support universal preschool for disadvantaged children, deregulation of overly restrictive educational policies, improved accountability, increased teacher professionalism, and greater resources for early childhood development and education. However, we do not believe that any one of these strategies on its own will do the job. Improving the development and education of all the nation's children will require a combination of these and other key strategies, a long-term commitment to the process of change, and the willingness and patience to see the job through.*

We call for a systematic reappraisal of the way our nation prepares children to become capable adults and urge the development of a comprehensive and coordinated human investment strategy for child development and education. Our nation must take on the difficult challenge of ensuring that all children have the opportunity to develop their fullest capacity for citizenship and productive work.

We believe that this approach to human investment is critical if we are to reduce the number of disadvantaged children and increase the chances that all children can productively participate in the mainstream of economic life. Solutions to the nation's educational problems that focus on the school system alone will continue to fail for two key reasons:

- Children born and reared in poverty generally suffer a multitude of debilitating health, emotional, social, and family problems that can impede learning. These children usually start school poorly prepared for formal schoolwork, and most school-based remedial strategies have proven less than successful in bringing them up to par. Once in school, many disadvantaged children fall farther and farther behind until poor performance, low self-esteem, alienation, and frustration cause them to drop out.

- The traditional school mission of teaching basic and advanced academic skills has generally been most successful when the student population is relatively similar in their level of preparation for school, when children's lives are reasonably stable and secure, and when families, educators, and the community have high expectations for their children and hold them to high standards. Where children's lives are chaotic, where parents feel alienated from the school system, where families and educators do not expect children to achieve, where communities do not support education, and where resources do not match needs, the traditional school model has failed to educate effectively. Nor are schools equipped to provide children with the emotional, physical, and moral support more appropriately provided by a stable, nurturing family.

---

*See memoranda by GEORGE C. EADS, (page 92).

Mounting societal pressures, not the least of which are the startling growth in the number of single-parent homes and an increase in childhood poverty, have forced public schools to assume responsibilities for the welfare of children that go well beyond their traditional educational mission. As a result, many public schools, particularly in urban areas but also in many suburban and rural communities, are increasingly pursuing a broad social agenda and are providing a wide range of social services, including free breakfast and lunch programs, health clinics, before- and after-school programs, and child care centers. Much of this activity is being pursued on an ad hoc basis in response to a crisis, and few schools have the financial resources, trained personnel, or administrative flexibility to fully address the increasing social-support needs of their students. With re-sources stretched thin, it is not surprising that in many schools neither the academic nor the social agenda is being fully realized.

Our public school systems and the institutions that support them must take a new look at the mission of public education in a rapidly changing society and develop strategies that will more effectively meet the goals we are in the process of setting for the nation's children. Public schools are the primary public institution charged with helping children prepare to be capable adults. As such, they have the responsibility for ensuring that their students learn by adapting to the children's changing circumstances and learning needs. To do this, the schools must have appropriate support and resources from the community at large. We believe that society must do two things simultaneously.

- First, the nation must redefine education as a process that begins at birth, recognizes that the potential for learning begins even earlier, and encompasses the physical, social, emotional, and cognitive de-velopment of children. Our public- and private-sector institutions, including the family, must do a better job of preparing children for formal schooling by ensuring that they are born healthy and receive the physical and emotional nurturing and intellectual stimulation necessary for successful early childhood development. The key goal should be to strengthen families, not to supplant them, and to help them do the best possible job of nurturing their children.

- Second, the schools must be better prepared to help children become educated no matter what their social, economic, or cultural background. Society must have a better understanding of both the academic and the social missions of the schools, and the schools should have the appropriate resources needed to carry out their responsibilities.

KEY IMPERATIVES FOR CHANGE

1. **The nation needs a comprehensive and coordinated human-investment strategy for child development and education that helps all children become productive citizens and self-sustaining adults.** The profound changes in family structure and stability coupled with the necessity for educating all children are forcing society to assume greater responsibility for the successful development and education of children. As a first step, every community should conduct a formal assessment of how it is addressing the needs of children, paying particular attention to the barriers that prevent change.

2. **Programs for assisting children should also help strengthen the entire family.** Family is central to every child's life, but when parents cannot give adequate care, especially young parents who may not have even basic parenting skills, society should provide the kind of support and assistance that will teach them to nurture their children and help strengthen their family.

3. **Every teen mother and father who has not finished high school should have access to a specialized school equipped to deal with the problems of teen parents and their children.** Teenage parenthood is a major cause of dropping out and family poverty. Programs designed along the lines of Albuquerque's New Futures School help teen parents develop the parenting, learning, and job skills they need while providing their children with developmentally appropriate early childhood education.

4. **Quality early childhood education should be available to all children who may not otherwise get adequate preparation for formal education from their families.** All children need to experience successful physical, social, emotional, and cognitive development to be able to embrace educational and social opportunities successfully. Whether called *child care, early childhood education,* or *preschool,* all programs for young children should be developmentally appropriate and focus on their educational needs. Public school systems should recognize the importance of early childhood education to their educational mission and help to ensure that quality programs are both available and accessible to all children who need them.

5. **Programs that address the needs of children and families must be flexible in design, administration, and funding.** Service providers often operate under crippling constraints and rigid funding dictated by federal and state governments that often prevent them from meeting the complex needs of the children and families they serve.

6. **Successful programs must be broadly replicated so that they are both more available and more accessible to all children in need and their families.** We know what works in education and child development, but few successful programs ever get past the pilot stage and seldom reach more than a small percentage of the children who need them.

7. **The mission of the public schools must be redefined to account for the changing requirements of society and the needs of children. Clearer goals and more effective methods of measurement are needed if the schools are to become more accountable for results.** Communities must reach a consensus on the appropriate social and educational roles of the public schools before school restructuring can take place. Business should work with educators, public officials, and other community leaders to develop goals for education and measures of performance that reflect the real skills and knowledge that students will need when they embark on their adult responsibilities.

8. **Students must be encouraged to take greater personal responsibility for the success of their own education.** Only someone who is actively engaged in the learning process will become an educated person. Business should work with educators, parents, and students themselves to provide greater incentives for students to work harder and learn better.

9. **Businesses should encourage their employees and other adults to volunteer in education and child development programs.** Volunteers are critical to the success of many programs that call for increased interaction between adults and children, such as mentoring and preschool. Business should also provide the training and support necessary to ensure a successful volunteer experience.

10. **Business should play a leadership role in identifying strategies for improving children's educational development and in determining what resources are needed to achieve results.** Although many of the changes in public policy and practice that are needed to improve child development and education will result in cost savings down the road, other essential improvements will initially require new investments. Business should lend its expertise to improving the management of existing resources and to achieving savings in other government programs that can be reallocated to the needs of children and schools. Where necessary, business should provide support for increasing the level of resources. State government should be the prime target of business involvement in policy, since most decisions on policy, practice, and funding in education and child development are made in state legislatures.

Some communities are already grappling with these issues. In Minneapolis, the Success by 6 project, developed by United Way and led by the corporate sector, is attempting to create a community where all children have the necessary mental, physical, social, and emotional development by age six to be able to embrace educational and social opportunities for growth and learning successfully. A number of other communities, including Milwaukee, Phoenix, Cincinnati, and Houston, are pursuing similar projects, and the United Way of America is exploring the possibility of replicating Success by 6 in selected cities around the nation.

Such comprehensive examples of institutional transformation are still rare. Most state and local education restructuring efforts maintain a narrow perspective on the nature of learning in childhood. As a result, they usually fail to recognize the direct connection between the health and development of infants and toddlers, the strength of their families, and their ability to become successful learners. Although many state and local restructuring plans recognize the importance of better preparing disadvantaged children for school, they continue to limit early childhood education to small pilot programs that bring children into schools for a few hours a day at age four to focus on academic acceleration. In addition, many such programs fail to encourage parent participation. More farsighted local communities and states such as Portland (Oregon), Seattle, New Jersey, Arizona, and Connecticut are increasingly making early childhood development and family support part of their overall human investment strategy.

RESPONDING TO A NEW DIVERSITY

Societal changes have hit the schools with full force in the past few years. Schools that were designed to educate a relatively stable student body are straining to adapt to students who are increasingly diverse, with great differences in racial and cultural heritage, language, health, family situation, and preparation for schooling. Over half of the nation's largest urban centers now have school populations that are predominantly black and Hispanic and who are more likely to be poor and from single-parent homes.[5]

There is every indication that the problems of children growing up in poverty are more acute today than they were in 1965 when the Great Society antipoverty programs such as Head Start were created. In 1989, nearly 11 percent of babies were born exposed to illegal drugs. Some hospitals report that up to 27 percent of women in their area are using illegal drugs during pregnancy.[6] Decent health care is becoming scarcer in poor areas, both urban and rural. What usually exists is emergency care; few preventive medical services are available in poorer communities. The consequences can be devastating. In New York's inner-city community of Harlem, the death rate among black males is higher than the death rate in many Third World countries.

One of the most serious demographic changes in the past two decades has been the alarming rise in poverty among young families, which are defined as those with a head of household who is under thirty. Such families have seen their rate of poverty increase from 12 percent in 1967 to over 21 percent in 1986. Families with very young heads of household (under twenty-five years of age) have seen their rate of poverty more than double in the same period, from 15.3 percent in 1967 to 32.6 percent in 1986.[7] Although a number of factors have contributed to this dramatic increase, one of the key causes has been the alarming increase in households headed by single women. In the past forty years, the rate of births to unmarried women in the United States has skyrocketed from less than 4 percent in 1950 to over 25 percent in 1988 (see Figure 1). According to the Grant

FIGURE 1

Births to Single Women, 1950 to 1988

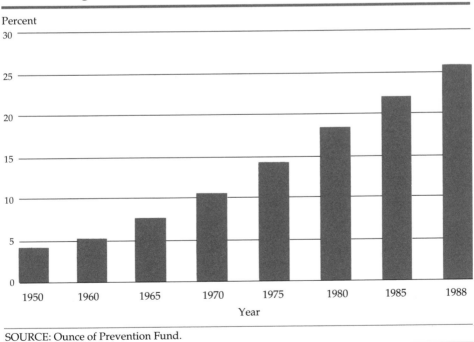

SOURCE: Ounce of Prevention Fund.

Commission, families headed by single women under the age of twenty-five who have dropped out of school are virtually guaranteed to be living in poverty. Furthermore, for a young, single woman with children, having a high school degree does not necessarily guard against poverty; in fact, nearly three-quarters of families headed by young single women who are high school graduates are living in poverty (see Figure 2).

Even in communities that are not poor, family resources are stretched, and new burdens are being placed on public-sector policies and business practices. More than half of mothers of children under age six are now in the work force. Families in which the father works and the mother stays at home while the children are in school account for only 8 percent of today's families.[8] A three-year-old in full-time child care from 8:00 a.m. until 6:00 p.m. spends about half of his waking hours in the care of adults other than his parents.

For school-age children who live in homes where all the adults work full time, a substantial part of the day may be spent without any adult guidance at all. Not only are growing numbers of preschool and school-age children spending less time under the direct supervision of a parent, but parents who work long hours outside the home have less time and energy

FIGURE 2

Poverty Rates of Young Families, by Age of Householder, as of March 1987 (in percentages)

Family Type	Householder Under 25	Householder 25-29
Married couple, headed by college graduate, no children	3.5	0.0
Married couple, headed by high school graduate, no children	3.5	2.0
Married couple, headed by high school graduate, one or more children	18.5	9.0
Married couple, headed by high school dropout, one or more children	36.5	24.7
Female-headed family, headed by high school graduate, one or more children	72.8	57.5
Female-headed family, headed by high school dropout, one or more children	92.6	81.5

SOURCE: *The Forgotten Half: Pathways to Success for America's Youth and Young Families.* Washington, D.C.: Youth and America's Future: The William T. Grant Commission on Work, Family, and Citizenship, November 1988.

to focus on their children's early development or schooling. The result is generally weaker connections among the family, the school, and the community, with more responsibility for child development and preparation for school falling on institutions outside the family.

THE HIGH COST OF FAILURE

Business people know that it is less expensive to prevent failure than to try to correct it later. Early intervention for poor children from conception to age five has been shown to be a highly cost-effective strategy for reducing later expenditures on a wide variety of health, developmental, and educational problems that often interfere with learning. Long-term studies of the benefits of preschool education have demonstrated returns on investment ranging from $3 to $6 for every $1 spent. Prenatal care has been shown to yield over $3.38 in savings on the costs of care for low-birthweight babies. Early immunization for a variety of childhood diseases saves $10 in later medical costs. Supplementing nutrition for poor women, infants, and children yields a $3 payback in savings on later health care costs.[9]

At the same time, the costs of not intervening early can be astronomical.

- Every "class" of dropouts earns about $237 billion less than an equivalent class of high school graduates during their lifetimes. As a result, the government receives about $70 billion less in tax revenues.

- Each year, taxpayers spend $16.6 billion to support the children of teenage parents.

- About 82 percent of all Americans in prison are high school dropouts, and it costs an average of $20,000 to maintain each prisoner annually. In comparison, a year of high-quality preschool costs about $4,800 and has been shown to decrease the rate of arrest in the teenage years by 40 percent.

REMOVING THE BARRIERS TO CHANGE

By its very nature, institutional change is slow and often painful for those who have been used to operating in the same way for decades. Even in large corporations, where lines of authority are easily defined, major restructuring can take a decade or more before targets are reached.

Public education itself is difficult to change because it is not one corporate entity but many. Public education in the United States is a $210

billion industry with 50 independent state bureaucracies that have jurisdiction over 16,000 quasi-independent local school districts, 84,000 schools,
and 4.2 million employees serving nearly 50 million pupils.

The public schools are not the only societal institutions that need to
be restructured. Education and child development policies have produced a crazy quilt of programs, often overlapping, uncoordinated, or
conflicting. They are created, regulated, and funded at every level of
government and administered by a multitude of public and private
agencies. Changes in these policies must also occur at every level, and in
order to be effective, such changes must be comprehensive and coordinated.

Coordination and collaboration among the many social and health
care agencies that should serve disadvantaged children are generally
poor or nonexistent. Community-based child care and early childhood
education programs also lack coordination or efficient systems for matching programs to the needs of children and parents. In most communities,
poor communications impede cooperation among the network of child
care providers, providers of family-support services, and the education
system.

The assessment of community needs conducted by Minneapolis
United Way for its Success by 6 project revealed that even in communities
that make extra efforts to meet the needs of families, parents can have
difficulty locating and obtaining quality early childhood services because
there is lack of consensus on how such services should best be delivered,
trained professionals are in short supply, coordination among service
providers is insufficient, and serious gaps in services remain. Other
barriers to restructuring include:

- Fragmented responsibility across the many different departments
  and agencies providing assistance to disadvantaged children and
  their families.

- Restrictive funding practices that force social service agencies to
  artificially categorize their clients and that prevent them from responding to the needs of children and families who often have
  multiple problems. At last count, the General Accounting Office
  (GAO) identified forty-six federal programs, not including Medi-
  caid, that provide funds for child care or related services.

- Difficulty in obtaining political support for services for disadvantaged children who may not have obvious physical handicaps but
  who may be at great risk because of poverty, discrimination, or
  neglect.

- Short-term funding for many pilot projects that frustrates efforts to focus on long-term gains.

- Competition between education and child development programs and other federal, state, and local budget priorities.

- Rigid assessment requirements that make it difficult to respond to unanticipated needs and opportunities.

- Low pay, difficult working conditions, and low esteem in which professionals in child care, early childhood education, and human services are held, making it difficult to attract and retain well-trained and qualified personnel in these fields. Without them, no program can be successful, no matter how well intentioned.

- Adversarial collective bargaining relationships between teacher and administrative unions and school districts.

We urge every community in the United States to conduct a comprehensive assessment of how it is addressing the needs of children. Such an assessment should be carried out by a broad coalition of interested groups, both public and private, and it should focus on community needs, existing programs and policies, coordination between early childhood development and education, and gaps in coverage. It should identify barriers to improvement and recommend strategies for removing those barriers.

INVESTING IN CHILD DEVELOPMENT AND EDUCATION

Restructuring education and child development policies may require major changes in legislation and practices at the state and federal levels, but it does not necessarily increase costs. Making some structural changes such as increasing program flexibility, coordinating programs across a variety of agencies, and reducing unnecessary regulations will ensure a more effective and efficient use of funds and is likely to save money in the long run.

But we should not fool ourselves into thinking that these savings will occur right away. The nation currently spends about $210 billion a year on elementary and secondary education, but per pupil expenditures can vary by as much as $8,000 between districts in the same state. Some needed improvements in child development and education will require new investments of resources, both financial and human. Among them are increasing the availability of prenatal care, quality child care, and preschool; increasing the salaries of child care workers and teachers; making long-postponed capital improvements in many older school facilities; and increasing the availability of computers and other advanced learning technologies.

We urge business to play a leadership role in identifying strategies for improving children's educational development and in determining

FIGURE 3

Funds Needed for Early Childhood Development of Poor Children

Programs	Cost (In Billions)
Prenatal care[a]	$ 0.56
WIC[b]	3.60
Childhood immunization[c]	0.08
Infant/toddler care[d]	
One- and two-year-olds	
880,000 full-day X $5,000	4.25
880,000 half-day X $4,000	3.55
Preschool[e]	
Three- and four-year olds	
888,000 full-day X $4,800	4.26
888,000 half-day X $3,640	3.23
Total funds required to ensure adequate development and early education of poor children	19.53
Federal funds currently allocated[f]	
WIC	2.35
Child care	5.00
Head Start	1.95
Total	9.30
Total new funds needed	$10.23

NOTES

[a]Estimate based on 3.9 million live births in 1988, of whom 24% were born to mothers who received no first trimester care, and average cost per client of $600 per client.

[b]Congressional Budget Office, September 1990. About half of those eligible are currently being served.

[c]Source: Children's Defense Fund, *S.O.S. America: A Children's Defense Budget*, page 74.

[d]Estimate based on number of births in 1988 surviving to age one multiplied by a 23% poverty rate for all children under age six. Assumption is that about half of these children would be enrolled in full-day and half in part-day programs.

[e]Program cost estimates from GAO report, *Early Childhood Education: What are the Costs of High-Quality Programs?*, January 1990, and Human Services Reauthorization Act of 1990, Senate Report 101421, August 1990. Total costs based on estimate of number of children in those age groups living in poverty using the 23% poverty rate for all children under age six.

[f]Includes 1991 appropriations for WIC, Head Start, and child care under a variety of federal child care programs, including the child care tax credit and pretax dependent care deduction.

what resources are needed to achieve results. Business should lend its expertise to improving the management of existing resources and achieving savings in other government programs that can be reallocated to the needs of children and schools. Where necessary, business should provide support for increasing the level of resources.

We believe that education is an investment, not an expense. If we can ensure that all children are born healthy and develop the skills and knowledge they need to be productive, self-supporting adults, whatever is spent on their development and education will be returned many times over in higher productivity, incomes, and taxes and in lower costs for welfare, health care, crime, and myriad other economic and social problems.

The potential for learning begins even before birth. The ability of children to succeed in school and in life is largely dependent on the quality of their early development. At a minimum, this means that the nation should provide adequate prenatal care to all mothers who cannot afford or do not have access to it, adequate preventive health care and nutrition support for poor children, quality child care for poor infants and toddlers, and quality preschool for disadvantaged three- and four-year-olds (see Figure 3). The additional cost of providing these services would total approximately $10.23 billion, which should be derived from a combination of federal, state, and local revenues and phased in over several years. This amount represents less than 5 percent of the nation's total outlay for elementary and secondary education. It is an investment we can ill afford to postpone.

* * *

Sustaining the momentum for change will not be easy. It will require a renewed commitment and the continued collaboration of every sector of society, including business, government, educators, civic leaders, parents, and the public, to marshal the political will necessary to transform the institutions that prepare our children for informed and productive citizenship.

We believe that it is more important than ever to act on the knowledge that our children are our future. If we fail to nurture and educate *all* our children, we will be closing the doors of opportunity to a growing number of young people and excluding them from participation in the mainstream of American life. The cost of failure is enormous, for what is at stake is the survival of our free-enterprise economy, our democratic system, and the American Dream itself.

Chapter 2

CHILD DEVELOPMENT AND EDUCATION: TOWARD A COMPREHENSIVE AND COORDINATED SYSTEM

Learning is a lifelong process that begins at birth. What children learn or fail to learn in their earliest years either helps to prepare them to become self-supporting adults or stunts their development and encourages dependency.

Whether formally or informally, children are learning all the time. Formal learning occurs through participation in traditional elementary, secondary, and higher education. Informal learning is the product of a child's interactions with the environment and the adults and peers within that environment. It occurs in a variety of settings: in the home, in the community, and through the mass media. In the first few years of life, what children learn and how well they learn it depend on the ability of parents and other caregivers to provide the nurturing, emotional stability, and intellectual stimulation they need to continue on a healthy course of development.

Children who are disadvantaged because of poverty, discrimination, neglect, or abuse often do not receive this crucial nurturing in their early years. Such children often arrive at school in poor health, developmentally delayed, socially maladjusted, physically handicapped, or simply unprepared for the rigors of formal schooling – conditions that sow the seeds of academic failure. The problems many disadvantaged children bring to the classroom can also take their toll on children who, by most standards, would be considered adequately prepared. Schools and individual teachers are often forced to address the deficits of disadvantaged children by paying less attention to the learning needs of the nondisadvantaged, thereby placing at risk a majority of children in those classrooms.

New research demonstrates that early intervention works. A recent four-year study of nearly 1,000 premature infants from birth through age three demonstrates that intensive early intervention with low-birthweight infants can significantly improve their chances for normal intellectual development. A control group of low-birthweight infants who received no intervention services were nearly three times more likely to have IQ scores in the range of mental retardation. The intensive intervention, which was led by Stanford University and funded by the Robert Wood Johnson Foundation, included regular home visits, parental training, and participation in child development centers.

In its 1987 policy statement, *Children in Need*, CED urged early and sustained intervention in the lives of disadvantaged children to help them break the cycle of failure and dependency and recommended a three-part strategy that includes early intervention and prevention, school restructuring, and retention and reentry programs for dropouts.

Although we believe an approach emphasizing intervention in early childhood is necessary for poor and otherwise disadvantaged children, we also believe that all children, not just those who are at the greatest risk of dropping out, would benefit from a more comprehensive and coordinated approach to education and child development.

All children in today's society are subject to increased stresses because of widespread changes in family life and growing pressure to succeed in school. Although the disadvantaged will need the most help and the most extensive and sustained interventions, we believe that more attention should be paid to the developmental needs of all children from conception through adolescence.

THE ROLE OF PARENTS

The role of parents in child development is paramount. Parents are responsible for providing for their children, nurturing them, and protecting them. In a very real sense, parents are their children's first and most important teachers. Under the best circumstances, parents show their children how the world works and provide the emotional security and intellectual stimulation children need for success in education and in life. A number of studies of values formation among teenagers have found that family values play a far more important role than the values of peers or other adults in the community. Unfortunately, when parents are unable to carry out their responsibilities toward their children, society is often left with the burden.

We believe that programs for assisting children should also help strengthen the entire family unit. When parents cannot care adequately for their children, especially young parents who may not have even basic parenting skills, society should provide the kind of support and assistance that will help reinforce the family and help parents learn to do a better job of nurturing their children.

Unfortunately, many parents who are young, poor, who experienced abuse or neglect in their childhoods, or who are otherwise living chaotic, socially isolated, and stress-filled lives are unable or unwilling to play this primary parental role. Most often, the will is there, but the parenting skills are underdeveloped or absent. Teenage parenthood is also a major cause of dropping out of school and long-term family poverty. If adequate prenatal care were provided where needed and if teenagers who are pregnant or already parents could be kept in school, the dropout rate could be substantially reduced. **We believe that every teen mother and father who has not finished high school should have access to a specialized school equipped to deal with the problems of teen parents and their children.**

ALBUQUERQUE'S NEW FUTURES SCHOOL

The New Futures School offers comprehensive educational, health, counseling, vocational, and child care services for pregnant teens and adolescent parents. An alternative school within the Albuquerque, New Mexico, public school system, New Futures School is supported by a nonprofit, community-based organization, New Futures, Inc.

The goal of the school is to help school-age parents make responsible, informed decisions, complete their education, have healthy babies, and become well adjusted and self-sufficient. Since its creation in 1970, New Futures School has provided services for more than 5,000 adolescent parents.

The program's in-school services are divided into two departments: the Perinatal Program, which serves the teen who enters the school during her pregnancy and remains until the end of the semester in which her child is born, and the Young Parent's Center, which is designed to serve the school-age mother who cannot successfully participate in a regular school program following the birth of her child.

The school offers a full range of support services, including health care and group and individual counseling. Health services include individual health counseling, group health instruction, nutrition counseling, and onsite health care provided by collaborating agencies.

The school operates four onsite child care facilities. In addition to providing child care for the mothers in school, these facilities provide the staff with an opportunity to observe the parenting skills of the young mothers, give mothers time to breast-feed, and provide experience for students in classes on child care and development.

SOURCE: The New Futures School.

Programs designed along the lines of Albuquerque's New Futures School help teen parents develop the parenting, learning, and job skills they need while providing their children with developmentally appropriate early childhood education (see page 18). In Minneapolis, Honeywell, Inc., as part of the Minneapolis Success by 6 program, has created in collaboration with the public schools a new high school for pregnant

---

MISSOURI'S PARENTS AS TEACHERS PROGRAM

The Parents as Teachers (PAT) parent-education program began in 1981 as a demonstration project sponsored by the Missouri Department of Elementary and Secondary Education. The program was designed to assess the value of providing high-quality parenting education for new parents for three years from the birth of their children. Services were provided to the 380 families enrolled in four districts with different socioeconomic profiles. Services included providing information on child growth and development, periodic developmental and health screening, monthly home visits by parent educators, and monthly group meetings at neighborhood parent resource centers.

When children in this pilot program reached age three, a randomly selected group was tested against a carefully matched comparison group. Results of this evaluation, conducted by an independent research firm, confirmed the benefits of the program. At age three, children in the pilot program were significantly more advanced in language and social development than other three-year-olds. They also made greater strides in problem solving and other intellectual skills that are important for later school success. The evaluation showed that both parents and children benefited from the program regardless of socioeconomic status and other traditional risk factors.

A four-year follow-up study of the families who took part in the PAT pilot program indicates that at the end of first grade, the PAT children are significantly more successful in school and parents play a more active role in their children's learning and formal schooling. Other major findings include:

- Significantly higher scores for PAT children on all measures of intelligence, achievement, auditory comprehension, verbal ability, and language ability.

- PAT children demonstrated more positive social development than non-PAT children. PAT parents reported that their children had a better developed sense of self, had more positive relationships with adults, and demonstrated better coping capabilities.

- Significantly more PAT parents initiated requests for parent-teacher conferences after their children started school.

SOURCE: Missouri Department of Secondary and Elementary Education.

teenagers and teen mothers. Modeled after New Futures, the Minneapolis school has been set up at Honeywell's headquarters building.

In many places around the country, a variety of intervention programs are having dramatic results in helping parents to improve their parenting skills and in strengthening the family unit. One of the best known is the Missouri Parents as Teachers program (PAT), which provides intensive education for parents with children from birth to age three. After the first three years, children in these families were more verbal and socially confident, and had better problem-solving skills than children whose parents did not participate. By the time the PAT children reached first grade, their academic performance was well ahead of their peers', and teachers reported that the PAT parents were more highly involved in their children's education than other parents were (see page 19).

THE KENAN TRUST FAMILY LITERACY PROJECT

The Family Literacy Project developed and sponsored by the Kenan Trust in the state of Kentucky is based on the premise that breaking the intergenerational cycle of illiteracy means more than just teaching reading; it means changing attitudes, values, and in some cases, cultures.

In the program, parents and children ride the school bus together, have breakfast at school together, and then attend separate three-hour classes in nearby classrooms. The parents work on basic academic skills – reading, math, and oral and written communication – all with an emphasis on critical thinking. Pre-vocational skills are taught to help parents plan for employment. During this same three hours, the children are in preschool classes using the High Scope curriculum. Afterwards, parents and children come together for Parents as Teachers Time, a forty-five-minute period of joint activities. After lunch together, the parents meet with teachers for parenting education while the children play. At the end of the school year, both parents and children receive diplomas and a $50 gift certificate to be redeemed at the local school-supply store.

After one year in the program, 85 percent of parents increased their academic aptitude scores by two or more grade levels or passed the general educational development (GED) exam, and children increased their developmental skills by 67 percent. In addition, parents learned faster than participants in other literacy programs and felt they were better equipped to meet their children's emotional and educational needs, helping them create a closer bond with their children.

SOURCE: *A Place to Start: The Kenan Trust Family Literacy Project*, September 1989.

Another program that is having excellent results in improving parental understanding of the importance of their children's education is the Family Literacy Program sponsored by the Kenan Trust throughout the state of Kentucky (see page 20).

CONNECTING FAMILIES TO SOCIAL SERVICES

Poor individuals and families tend to have multiple and interrelated problems and complex needs. Lack of money often means that living conditions are poor because housing that is both available and affordable is substandard; health problems are common because of poor nutrition or environmental hazards caused by substandard living conditions; the family head is overburdened and has few coping skills; the bureaucracy is intimidating; forms are difficult to fill out because parents lack basic literacy skills.

Such multiple-problem families need help in determining what services they need, assistance in finding and gaining access to those services, and support to help them successfully utilize those services.

One obstacle to connecting multiple-problem families to the range of services they need is that funding for most federal and state services is categorical. Program guidelines contain extensive regulations and restrictions on how funds may be used. This forces people with few coping skills to deal with multiple agencies and service providers in order to meet basic family needs. An individual service provider may identify the client's other problems not addressed by his or her agency, but few can go beyond simple referrals. Obtaining the other services is entirely up to the person in need.

This categorical view of social services is slowly changing. Federal and state policies are beginning to reflect the need for increased flexibility in funding and better coordination among services. For example, the Family Support Act of 1988 is attempting to coordinate education and jobs-training programs for parents with child care services for their children. New Federal special education legislation requires states to establish interagency councils to coordinate programs for handicapped infants and toddlers. And the McKinney Act, which provides funds for the homeless, also requires states to establish interagency planning as a condition for obtaining federal funds.

A second obstacle is the inflexible way in which federal funds are often disbursed to state and local programs. Often, such rigid guidelines can subvert the intended purpose of encouraging better collaboration. For example, in interpreting the rules for disbursing funds under the jobs and training provision of the Family Support Act, the U.S. Department of Health and Human Services has required that unless all dollars allocated for jobs are funneled through the state welfare agency, a state could lose federal matching funds. This requirement makes its difficult, if not impossible, for many states to coordinate program funding among a variety of education, labor, and other agencies where funds may be more effectively utilized.

A third obstacle is the sheer number of public and private agencies involved in providing services, which leads to overlap, confusion, and lack of flexibility in meeting needs. For example, California has 160 programs serving children and youths that are overseen by 37 different entities located in seven different state departments. However, the governor of California recently acted to remedy this situation by creating a cabinet-level department to coordinate all child development and education programs.

A fourth obstacle is that the design of many services is inadequate for solving the full problem. If services are available but inadequate, they will probably fail to deliver on their promises. The mere presence of child and family services is insufficient; both their *content* and their *quality* are critical for success. One reason is that people in poverty rarely have single problems that can be easily addressed through simple strategies. They usually face multiple problems, are poorly informed, and are intimidated by large bureaucracies.

Prenatal care is a good example of the kind of intervention strategy that should be carefully tailored to meet the needs of the women who will benefit from it. Conventional prenatal care that is adequate for the needs of an educated, middle-class woman will not be sufficient for the inner-city pregnant teenager who is depressed, not eating properly, and perhaps drinking and taking drugs and who may not have a permanent home. She needs earlier identification and more highly sustained intervention to ensure that she delivers a healthy baby and learns how to care for it properly.

Likewise, if it costs $4,800 a year for the kind of high-quality, comprehensive preschool program that we know yields long-term results, spending only $2,700 per child, which is the average Head Start allocation, will not result in the same gains for the child over the long term, largely because different costs reflect different program components.

Programs that successfully address the multiple problems of at-risk children and families have a number of common characteristics:[1]

- They are comprehensive, coherent, integrated, and flexible.

- They cross traditional bureaucratic and professional boundaries.

- They deal with the child as part of the family and the family as part of the community.

- They make sure that staff members have the time, training, and skills necessary to build relationships of trust and respect with children and families.

- They design the content of their services to address the special needs of the people they are serving.

Numerous examples of such comprehensive programs have demonstrated improved long-term results for children and their families. Many of these programs use case-management techniques, in which the practitioner assigned to a particular family identifies problems and coordinates the services it needs. In a semirural area of upstate New York, which has the highest child abuse rate in the state, the Elmira Prenatal/Early Infancy Project (PEIP) offered comprehensive home-visiting services to 400 high-risk women expecting their first child. Most of the women were teenagers, unmarried, jobless, or on welfare. Registered nurses with special training paid nine home visits to each participant during the prenatal period. They tried to help mothers understand how their behavior affects the child, helped prepare them for childbirth, and discussed the mothers' future plans. After the births, the nurse continued visiting until the children were two years old. The results of the program were dramatic. Compared with a control group that received no home-visiting services, those receiving full intervention services experienced one-fifth as many cases of verified child abuse and neglect and the poor unmarried women returned to school more quickly, were employed more, obtained better child care, and had fewer pregnancies over the next four years.[2]

One particularly promising approach to providing intensive intervention services is the Comprehensive Child Development Centers (CCDC), which are modeled after ideas developed in the Parent-Child Development Centers of Head Start and the Beethoven Project in Chicago (see page 24). The CCDC program will provide more than $20 million in each of the next five years for more than 20 pilot centers that provide early, continuous, and comprehensive services to low-income families with infants and children.

Programs that address the needs of children and families should be flexible in design, administration, and funding. We urge federal and state policy makers to broaden the application of these principles to programs designed to improve the lives of disadvantaged children and families.

THE BEETHOVEN PROJECT

For the past three years, the Center for Successful Child Development (CSCD), popularly known as the Beethoven Project, has offered comprehensive services to children and their families in the Robert Taylor Homes, the largest and one of the poorest public housing projects in the nation.

The Beethoven Project is encouraged by the real opportunities for successful outcomes for these highly disadvantaged children. The program has also provided valuable insights about the realities of translating research on early intervention into action.

The single greatest challenge for the Beethoven Project staff has been to earn the trust of the mothers and their families. Without this trust, the staff cannot be effective in convincing mothers to obtain prenatal care that leads to healthier babies. As a result, CSCD is expanding training opportunities for paraprofessionals so they can be more effective in reaching out to these young women.

Prenatal care and parenting education are only the beginning of interventions that must be sustained to be successful. Even though a variety of services, including pediatric health care, a family drop-in center, infant and toddler developmental child care, Head Start, and special programs for teen parents, have been set up in the Robert Taylor Homes, they are often underutilized. CSCD continues to develop aggressive outreach efforts. One sign of success is that program participants themselves have become invaluable recruiters of new families.

One of the most successful aspects of the program is the primary health care center, which is supported by a five-year grant from the Robert Wood Johnson Foundation. More than 500 children have been treated. The pediatric nurse-practitioner provides basic well-child care, school physicals, and care of children with minor illnesses; and the medical director, who is a pediatrician, sees patients twice a week. The medical staff and the rest of the CSCD staff maintain constant communication.

The fact that the services are housed in one of the project buildings has been a mixed blessing. The staff has seen and, to some extent, experienced what life is like amid acute and chronic deprivation, violence, and isolation. They have shared the urgency of the relentless demands confronting these families. At times, their focus has been diverted from infant and child development concerns to immediate adult crises. The CSCD staff has learned it must serve the child first, without ignoring the families' needs. The commitment to better child development has been bolstered, along with more comprehensive services for the entire family. There are plans for programs aimed at literacy, substance-abuse prevention, and employability.

SOURCE: Ounce of Prevention Fund.

SCHOOLS AS A BASE FOR DELIVERING SERVICES

For school-age children and their families, the school itself can provide a convenient institutional focus for making this linkage because it is the one institution to which almost all children between five and seventeen have access. By addressing the needs of the child in school, service providers can also establish links with parents and other siblings who may not yet be in school or who may have already dropped out. Providing or coordinating services at schools can help school staffs gain new insights into the problems of students and can give faculties a new perspective on academic policies that have a negative impact on students. For example, in one Chicago school, the counselors in the Youth Guidance program became convinced that a particular school's suspension policy was counterproductive to the goal of keeping troubled young people in school. As a result, they helped school officials develop an alternative education program that better served the needs of students. In another case, the service coordinator brought a helpful perspective to an academic committee developing changes in the way English was taught to immigrant students.[3]

One of the nation's oldest models for service coordination within schools is the national Cities in Schools program. Currently operating in over 216 local communities, Cities in Schools provides a useful model for assessing the needs of children that go beyond what the school can normally provide and for bringing the requisite services, case managers, and counselors to the school site or, in some cases, establishing an alternative school, such as Rich's Academy in Atlanta, which focuses on the educational, social service, and employment needs of students (see page 26).

A number of states are beginning to expand on this model. New Jersey, for example, has established one of the most comprehensive experiments in school-based service delivery. Begun in 1988, the program now serves twenty-nine sites, with at least one in each county. Each center must provide five basic services: mental health and family counseling, health and substance-abuse services, employment counseling and training services, information and referral services, and recreation. In addition, each site may establish a program unique to the needs of its students. At South Brunswick High School, the Teen Center attracts 300 students a week to its year-round program of recreational and academic activities. Under this program, South Brunswick has begun a project to employ high school students as tutors of elementary school students.

Kentucky is the first state to establish a statewide network of family support programs within its schools as part of its broad education reform agenda (see page 78). The purpose of this initiative is to increase the capacity of families to support their children in school by linking them with the community services they need. The network, which is being developed with the assistance of the national Family Resource Coalition, will consist of family resource and youth centers that will operate in elementary and secondary schools with a substantial proportion of low-income students.

Despite the obvious advantages of using the neighborhood school as a base for providing social services – and the fact that it is already occurring – this is not necessarily the most appropriate strategy for all schools or communities. Nevertheless, whether a community decides to base its delivery system in the local school or at a different site, what will be necessary is greater flexibility in program design and funding to allow services to be provided in a coordinated manner.

CITIES IN SCHOOLS

For over twenty years, the national organization Cities in Schools, Inc. (CIS), has worked at the local level to bring a variety of social services to children at risk by focusing on each child's needs, building personal relationships with counselors and peers, and helping them to respond to the many forces that conspire to keep them from finishing school. Its dropout-prevention programs operate in forty-six communities across the country, serving almost 30,000 children at 216 sites.

CIS has developed partnerships with business to establish alternative schools around the country, such as Rich's Academy in Atlanta and the Burger King Academies, and it is also collaborating with other national organizations to expand their programs nationwide. United Way of America is linking CIS with local United Ways to provide CIS entry to new communities, and the Boys Clubs of America and CIS developed partnerships in thirty communities in 1990.

The most recent CIS initiative is its collaboration with BellSouth Foundation to expand its operations statewide beginning in four states in BellSouth's region: North Carolina, South Carolina, Georgia, and Florida. Each of the state offices will be responsible for promoting the CIS concept and replicating local CIS programs throughout the state; establishing relationships with appropriate state government agencies charged with addressing at-risk youth and dropout issues; working with the state government to create legislative change and reallocate resources; providing training to local CIS school-site teams; raising funds; overseeing implementation and evaluation of the program; and maintaining links with other CIS state boards and CIS national headquarters.

SOURCE: Cities in Schools, Inc.

A CASE-MANAGEMENT APPROACH

Case management offers a rational and cost-effective way to coordinate services for families and children with multiple problems. It is aimed at linking the service system with the consumer and coordinating the various system components to achieve a successful outcome. It is a problem-solving strategy that attempts to ensure continuity and coordination of services for individual clients.

Case management is not the only answer for ministering to the needs of at-risk children, youths, and families. It is difficult to implement, time-consuming, takes considerable resources to operate well, and depends on the willingness of established institutions to change their long-standing ways of doing business.

Nevertheless, case management can provide an essential measure of coordination and support for families and children in need of assistance. And as human service professionals confront increasingly complex problems and seek new ways to respond, case management can provide a valuable conceptual framework in which services can be planned and new techniques developed for bringing those plans into action.

THE EDUCATION AND CARE OF YOUNG CHILDREN

What children experience during the first five years is critical to their later educational success. Yet, policy makers have generally considered child care and early childhood education separate entities with different purposes and goals. The purpose of early childhood education is generally viewed as something profitable for society because it helps poor children succeed better in school. Child care, on the other hand, is often seen more as a benefit to parents, rather than children, so that the parents can go to work. In the past, this attitude has been particularly harmful to the children of mothers who were trying to get off welfare. Although the child care available to them could and often did provide programs fostering the children's social, emotional, and educational development, the financial support available for these programs generally provided for only custodial care.

This separation between early childhood education and child care is counterproductive. There are now many more disadvantaged children who need both early education and care, as well as more children of all economic circumstances who spend nearly as much time in the care of others as they do with their parents. We believe that it is necessary to narrow the gap between education and care for the sake of the healthy development and later educational needs of all children. **All programs for children from birth to age five – whether designated as child care, early** childhood education, or preschool – should focus on their educational and developmental needs. All early childhood education programs should be developmentally appropriate and take into account what children will need to succeed in school and in life.

PRESCHOOL AND EARLY CHILDHOOD EDUCATION

Quality preschool programs clearly provide one of the most cost-effective strategies for lowering the dropout rate and helping at-risk children to become more effective learners and productive citizens. It has been shown that for every $1 spent on a comprehensive and intensive preschool program for the disadvantaged, society saves up to $6 in the long-term costs of welfare, remedial education, teen pregnancy, and crime.

A recent evaluation of the New York City preschool program Project Giant Step confirms the positive impact of a high-quality preschool experience for disadvantaged children on their later school performance. Like Head Start, on which it is modeled, Project Giant Step provides developmentally appropriate education, encourages a high level of parent involvement, and offers comprehensive health and social services (see page 29).

The federally-funded Head Start program is the major program of its type, combining an intensive preschool experience with a comprehensive array of services geared to the needs of disadvantaged children and their families. In 1990, strong support for Head Start from a coalition of business, education, and government leaders culminated in historic legislation authorizing full funding for all eligible three- to five-year-olds by 1994 (see pages 36-38 for a discussion of the future of Head Start).

Many of the states have recognized the benefits of early intervention and are now placing a high priority on early childhood education for at-risk children, with thirty-five states currently funding preschool programs. The National Governors' Association and the White House have strongly endorsed preschool for its long-term economic and social benefits, and a call for universal preschool for at-risk children is part of the national goals for education issued in 1990.

Despite this universal enthusiasm, only about one-third of all poor three- and four-year-olds attend some form of preschool, and high-income families are twice as likely to enroll their children in an organized child care program with an educational component than low-income families are. Quality also varies widely among programs. Few states offer full-day programs or have the broad range of integrated health and family services that are a hallmark of Head Start. And despite the need for quality child care for parents in poverty who are trying to finish their education or to gain a foothold in the work force, few preschool programs for at-risk children incorporate full-day, developmentally based child care.

We believe that early childhood education should be available to all children who may not otherwise get adequate preparation for formal education from their families. States and local communities should

PROJECT GIANT STEP: PRESCHOOL IN NEW YORK CITY

In 1986, New York City created Project Giant Step to provide a half-day comprehensive public preschool program for low-income children. Administered jointly by New York City's Board of Education and the Agency for Child Development and taking place in both public schools and child care settings, Project Giant Step combines preschool education for the children with intensive support systems for the parents. The first study on the effects of Giant Step, conducted by Abt Associates of Cambridge, Massachusetts, found some promising results. The sample consisted of 1,077 children, and evaluative measures were developed in three areas: child development, parent and family characteristics and attitudes, and staff satisfaction.

Child Development. The program's educational component consists of three hours of classroom experience, either mornings or afternoons, five days a week, ten months a year. The half-day program has more than twice as great an impact on children's performance in cognitive tests as that of other early childhood programs serving similar populations, including Head Start. The study also found large gains in social and emotional development.

Effects on Parents. The program was successful in involving parents in educational activities and in their children's learning. Eighty percent of parents volunteered in the classroom and accompanied children on field trips. Seventy percent attended education classes or events organized by the program. Program staff also provided parents with information about health care, child care, employment services, and food assistance.

Staff Satisfaction. Giant Step has been successful in recruiting, training, and retaining highly qualified personnel. Giant Step staff turnover was only half that of other early childhood teaching staff nationally. Staff members were satisfied with the training they received in Giant Step and with the program itself and expressed their commitment to its success.

SOURCE: *Evaluation of Project Giant Step Year Two Report: The Study of Program Effects*, Executive Summary by Jean I. Layzer, Barbara D. Goodson, and Judith A. Layzer, Abt Associates Inc.

make early childhood education a more integral part of the formal education process, particularly in communities with large numbers of poor, non-English-speaking, or otherwise disadvantaged children. Public schools should recognize the importance of early childhood education to their educational mission and should help to ensure that programs are both available and accessible and relate well to the later educational needs of children.

In many communities, the public school system itself may offer the most cost-efficient institution for administering a broad-scale early childhood program. One example is the Ysleta Pre-Kinder Center in El Paso, Texas (see below). Public school systems already have mechanisms for reaching the vast majority of children in a community. Many systems currently have underutilized facilities because of changes in school populations or have the capability of mobilizing the resources needed to build new facilities.

However, in other communities, the public schools may not necessarily be the best institution to administer early childhood programs. If a

---

YSLETA PRE-KINDER CENTER

One example of a successful preschool program run by a public school system is the Ysleta Pre-Kinder Center in El Paso, Texas. Ysleta was established in 1985 in response to the 1984 education reform legislation in Texas that provided funding for half-day preschool programs for all four-year-olds who were either non-English-speaking or from a low-income family.

An informal survey of the elementary school teachers of the first children to go through the program indicates that the Ysleta children are better adjusted, better at following directions, and better able to cope with elementary school than children who did not have benefit of the program.

In Ysleta's first five years, the number of children served has jumped from 660 to 1,500 per year, and there are now three additional program sites. The program has been expanded to include a computer lab and a full-time librarian. Children are sent home with books to encourage parents to read to them. Ysleta has also expanded its volunteer program to include high school student interns and early childhood education students who serve as teachers' aides while doing their student teaching. In the next few years, Ysleta plans to hire a fine arts and drama teacher and a music teacher.

SOURCE: Ysleta Pre-Kinder Center.

school or school system is already doing a poor job of providing education to students from kindergarten to twelfth grade, or if its staff feels overwhelmed by the current tasks it has to perform, it is doubtful that the school system can successfully incorporate effective programs for preschoolers. In communities where the local public school system is overburdened or judged ineffective, a variety of nonprofit agencies such as churches and community-based organizations that already have experience running quality child care programs could provide an appropriate and effective institutional focus for preschool programs. In most communities, some combination of public school and community-based programs will provide the most effective and appropriate use of resources for early childhood education. State education authorities should assume the task of providing local communities with necessary funding, flexible guidelines, and appropriate oversight to ensure program quality.

EARLY CHILDHOOD CARE

From birth, children need quality care from their parents and other caregivers that contributes to their ability to learn and their readiness for school. For many parents who must work, the lack of availability of quality child care that is developmentally appropriate, has educational value, and is affordable has created a crisis of national proportions that affects most families but hits low-income families the hardest.[4] The recent National Child Care Staffing Study demonstrates that the high staff turnover rates and generally low quality of care provided in many child care centers are compromising the healthy development of large numbers of children, even middle-class children, whose parents cannot afford alternatives.

Child care in the United States is best characterized by its diversity. It is delivered in a variety of settings, including in the home by parents, other relatives, or paid nannies; in family child care homes generally run by neighborhood women; and in a wide range of community-based, for-profit, and school-based centers by child care workers or certified early childhood teachers. Although none of these methods is intrinsically better than any other, individual programs vary considerably in the quality of care provided, which can have a serious impact on the development and education of children.

According to the National Child Care Staffing Study, children in centers with lower-quality care and high staff turnover were less competent in language and social development, key indicators of later learning problems. The study, which examined 227 centers in five U.S. metropolitan areas, found that the most significant indicators of program quality were a high ratio of staff to children and a high level of staff education and training, which led to more positive adult-child interactions. Teaching staff provided more sensitive and appropriate care if they had completed more years of formal education, received early childhood training at the college level, earned higher wages, and received better benefits.

Most of the centers studied fell far below acceptable standards of quality, with high staff turnover the key reason. Despite having higher levels of formal education than the average American worker, child care teachers earn abysmally low wages. In 1988, their average hourly wage was $5.35, and between 1977 and 1988, child care staff inflation-adjusted wages decreased by more than 20 percent while staff turnover nearly tripled, from 15 to 41 percent. The lower the wages, the greater the likelihood that a child care worker would leave his or her position.

THE NEEDS OF POOR PARENTS. For many poor parents, particularly teens, who generally drop out of school when they have a child, access to quality child care is often critical to their further education, training, and employment. For such parents, quality care can help open the door to work and an independent life free from welfare. Yet poor parents face a number of major obstacles in obtaining quality care for their children. These include cost; limited access to information on the availability of services; and poor linkage of child care to other family support services, which may include education and training of parents, home visiting, parenting education and support programs, medical care, and nutrition assistance.

CHILD CARE AND WELFARE REFORM. The Family Support Act (FSA), which was passed by Congress in 1988, was designed in recognition of the need to provide child care for parents who are attempting to get off welfare by participating in education and training programs. The act is designed to strengthen the nation's child support enforcement system; help welfare recipients move into the labor market, primarily through participation in state education and training programs; and provide support services to facilitate that transition. Under FSA, parents are guaranteed child care assistance during their participation in approved education and training activities and for a period of 12 months after they become ineligible for benefits under Aid to Families with Dependent Children (AFDC) because of income from employment. The federal government will reimburse the states for a share of the child care expenses; the minimum is 60 percent. In addition, FSA requires that child care be coordinated with Head Start and other existing early childhood programs.

This act offers a promising approach, but its success will depend on how well participating states can comply with federal guidelines on providing access to good-quality care. Although the bill is designed to encourage parents to select child care that follows state and local quality guidelines, it does not require parents to use state-licensed or state-registered settings.

Early program results indicate that states are running into problems balancing the costs of implementing FSA with other necessary social services. Massachusetts and Minnesota may have to eliminate child care subsidies to the working poor, perhaps forcing some to go on welfare. In Orange County, California, 3,000 children of the working poor are on waiting lists for subsidized care, and the new welfare law will add 6,000 additional children to the list.

THE NEEDS OF WORKING PARENTS. For working parents, finding child care that is affordable, accessible, and of good quality is critical if they are to work productively without having to worry about their children's welfare during the day. Despite the pressing need for better child care among families of all income levels, particularly those at the bottom, the United States has only just begun to address the nation's child care needs with the recent passage of major child care legislation. In contrast, France has developed a comprehensive system that focuses on the educational and developmental needs of young children and on the concerns of working parents (see page 34). However, the child care legislation passed by Congress in late 1990 begins to address a number of key issues. The legislation provides increased federal monetary support for poor and low-income families to help meet child care needs, including $1.5 billion over five years to states for the purpose of providing child care to families that need to work to stay off welfare and expansion of the earned-income tax credit for low-income working families with children. The legislation also provides a new refundable tax credit to cover certain health insurance expenses of families with children. Equally important, the legislation requires states to establish health and safety standards for child care providers and to offer consumer education to parents to help them select child care; it also allows some funds to be used by states to address quality issues.

Out of necessity, employers have begun to help fill the child care gap for their employees. Employers have discovered that providing child care is a benefit that can help them both attract and retain qualified personnel. As a consequence, the number of companies providing child care assistance has more than doubled in three years, from 2,500 in 1986 to 5,400 in 1989. Nevertheless, this represents only a small fraction of all American employers, most of whom employ fewer than fifty people each and view child care as too expensive.[5]

The benefits that accrue to companies that provide child care assistance include improved recruitment and retention of employees, higher employee morale, and better community relations.

Some companies are reluctant to establish on-site child care because of possible liability problems. However, on-site care is only one of several

---

MEETING THE NEEDS OF CHILDREN IN FRANCE

The experience of France in developing a national child care system provides an instructive example of how another industrialized nation views the importance of early childhood development. The French system is based on the belief that every child benefits from working and playing cooperatively with other children under skilled adult supervision. They point to national census data showing that children of whatever social class have a better chance of passing first grade – a critical indicator of later school success – if they have attended preschool.

Recognizing that most parents cannot afford the full cost of quality child care, the French government has chosen to subsidize the portion that exceeds parents' means. Nearly 80 percent of the cost of child care is covered by public funds.

Free preschools serve nearly 90 percent of all three-, four-, and five-year-olds, and publicly subsidized private schools serve the remainder. Several types of infant-toddler care are available, including centers, family child care networks, and independent licensed family child care providers.

Teachers and other professional staff are aggressively recruited and receive intensive training. All preschool teachers and directors have training equivalent to a master's degree in early childhood and elementary education. Directors of infant-toddler programs are pediatric nurses who have professional training in public health, child development, and administration.

An extensive national service of preventive health care for mothers and their infants has reduced France's infant mortality rate to the world's eighth lowest. (By contrast, the U.S. ranks nineteenth.) Systematic links between health care services and children's programs help ensure that every child in infant-toddler and preschool care receives regular preventive health care.

France spends $7.12 billion annually (approximately $130 per capita) on its publicly sponsored child care and education, which includes $5 per capita spent on preventive maternal and infant health care and on health services linked with child care programs.

SOURCE: *A Welcome for Every Child: How France Achieves Quality in Child Care,* A Report of the French-American Foundation, New York, 1989.

options available to companies that want to help employees address this need. Companies can elect to become members of child care consortia, can provide financial assistance in the form of tax-free employee deductions or direct subsidies, or can implement resource and referral programs that provide parents with assistance in finding child care programs. Some companies are helping to upgrade the skills of family child care providers. The "Family-to-Family" initiative of Mervyn's Department Stores focuses on increasing the quality of family child care by supporting training and accreditation of caregivers as well as public awareness of quality for parents and policy makers. Launched in 1988 by Mervyn's, Target Stores, and the Dayton Hudson Foundation, the almost $10 million initiative will fund projects in 30 communities over seven years.

TARGETING ASSISTANCE. Although there are few families today who would not benefit from quality child care, any government subsidy should first target the needs of high-risk families, particularly those on public assistance and the working poor. These are the families that have the fewest economic and political resources and whose children are usually in greatest need of high-quality out-of-home care.

Any government action should support the basic principle that effective child care for disadvantaged families needs to be developmentally appropriate and should afford parents access to a range of related services. Some ways to accomplish this include the following:

- **Expand and supplement Head Start and other developmental preschool programs.** Most Head Start programs are half-day, which means that working parents whose children participate must still scramble to find adequate care for the rest of the day. In addition to serving more eligible children, Head Start should accommodate the hours of parents who are working or are in education or job-training programs. Existing programs that provide full-day care for infants and toddlers should be helped to improve their services so that they better meet these children's developmental needs.

- **Find new sources and methods of funding public programs.** Existing levels and sources of funding cannot provide enough money to assure that the working poor and welfare parents in school or training can afford quality child care. Eligibility for subsidies should be designed to avoid giving parents disincentives to participate in paid employment.

- **Help parents to become partners in their children's education and development.** A key component of developmentally based child care for disadvantaged families is parent education and support to help parents learn better nurturing skills.

- **Insist on appropriate training for center-based child care workers and implement training programs for home-based family child care providers.** One of the predictors of the quality and effectiveness of teachers in preschool programs is the amount of training they receive in early childhood development and education. Providing easily accessible community-based training for relatives who care for children or others who run family-based care facilities in their homes would also help to improve the overall quality of child care.

THE FUTURE OF HEAD START

The acknowledged effectiveness of Head Start has generated an unprecedented amount of attention and support in the past few years. In both *Investing in Our Children* and *Children in Need*, CED enthusiastically endorsed the program and called for full funding. And in historic legislation adopted in 1990, Congress authorized full funding by 1994. Nevertheless, the actual appropriation for 1991 is $1.952 billion, a $400 million increase over the 1990 appropriation but only half of the increase the legislation authorized. The significant funding increases in both 1990 and 1991 will enable Head Start to reach up to one-third of all eligible three- and four-year-olds, as well as five-year-olds not in kindergarten. In addition to full-funding targets, the 1990 Head Start reauthorization contains a number of important provisions for improving program quality, implementing transitional projects to help children sustain Head Start gains in elementary school, and expanding family support services and services to children from birth to age three.

CED continues to support full funding of Head Start to increase enrollment of all eligible three- to five-year-olds, and we urge Congress to follow through with appropriations that will match the full-funding authorization targets by 1994. We also believe that it is equally important that Congress promote the effectiveness of Head Start by ensuring adequate funds for maintaining the quality of services in both new and existing programs.

A hallmark of the Head Start program has always been a high level of parental involvement in day-to-day operations. Parents help direct the program and make up a substantial proportion of the teaching staff. Many parents who began as Head Start aides have eventually returned to school for their high school and even college degrees.

At a time of increasing employment among parents, Head Start has been moving away from directly meeting the extended-day needs of working families. Although the number of children served by Head Start has not changed appreciably in a decade, the percentage of full-day programs has declined from one-third in 1972 to about 15 percent in 1989. Furthermore, even programs characterized as full-day may meet for less than a full working day, fewer than five days a week, or fewer than twelve months a year. Only 6 percent of Head Start children are in nine-hour-per-day programs. Despite these trends, a 1988 study showed that 32 percent of Head Start parents were working full time and that another 19 percent worked part time, had seasonal jobs, or were in school or training programs. Lack of such full-day services is a barrier to enrollment of some families because parents often cannot arrange care or transportation for the remaining portion of the day.[6]

The positive results of such programs as the Perry Preschool Project and the Harlem Head Start Study derived from their intensity and comprehensiveness and from the highly trained staffs they provided. Although preschool for disadvantaged three- and four-year-olds is a critical cost-effective strategy for later school success, for a large proportion of poor children, even this intervention is too late. Even the most intensive programs at this age fail to help at least one-third of the children who participate. Important new research indicates that the longer a child attends preschool, the better his or her chances of starting school fully prepared. A study of over 4,500 preschoolers found that children identified as at risk of failure in first grade who have participated in at least three years of preschool were as prepared for school as children not deemed at risk. At the same time, for at-risk children with only one or two years of preschool, disparities in school readiness were pronounced.[7] Improvements in Head Start should include the following:

- Expand the comprehensive model of Head Start services to children from birth to age three so that their chances for a productive life can be improved as early as possible.

- Increase compensation and training of Head Start teachers and other staff. The average Head Start teacher earns less that $10,000 per year, and employee benefits such as health insurance and pensions are largely nonexistent.

- Broaden income eligibility to allow children of parents who are in transition into the work force to remain in the program as family income rises above the poverty level. Such families still need extensive support services to help them achieve stability.

- Allow greater flexibility in the use of funds to make it easier for Head Start to work in conjunction with state and local preschool, child care, and other early intervention programs.

In addition, Head Start should provide more full-day services that correspond to parents' work or school hours and the local flexibility to enable Head Start and child care services to be fully integrated as part of the Family Support Act.

Finally, the federal government should provide incentives for states and localities to use the comprehensive model of Head Start in designing preschool programs, work more cooperatively with the local Head Start programs, and where appropriate, expand services to at-risk children by supplementing Head Start funding.

Chapter 3

RESTRUCTURING SCHOOLS FOR THE 21st CENTURY

At the same time that we prepare children better for school, schools must be better prepared to educate all children to their fullest potential. Until recently, schools were not expected to develop the intellectual capacity of more than a limited segment of society. This is no longer the case. Our nation desperately needs schools that can help all children develop the skills and knowledge they need in a more competitive economy and a more complex world.

Our expectations for schools have changed radically, but for the most part the schools have not. Most children still attend schools that were designed for an agrarian and early industrial society. But what the nation needs now are schools that will prepare young people for a knowledge-based information age.

Ensuring that all children, particularly the disadvantaged, receive better preschool preparation is only half the battle. If we fail to ensure that these same children obtain a quality education that equips them to succeed in the modern world, we will have failed them and squandered our resources.

Schools need to be radically restructured to better prepare students for the challenges ahead by improving the way they deliver education and encourage children to learn. Nevertheless, restructuring education is not so much an end product as it is a process for bringing about change. Not every child learns in the same way or has the same educational needs. Accordingly, there should be a reasonably wide variation in what restructured schools look like: how they are organized, managed, staffed, what subjects are taught, and the pedagogical methods used. What restructured schools will have in common, however, will be education that is more effective and efficient and produces better outcomes for both students and society. Students will have the skills they need to function effectively in the workplace and in life. Society will benefit from a more skilled and knowledgeable work force and an informed and intelligent citizenry.

Underlying any attempt to restructure the schools, whether on the state or the local level, must be a clear understanding of the role of schools in today's society. **We believe that the mission of the public schools must be redefined to account for the changing requirements of society and the needs of children. Communities must first reach a consensus on the appropriate social and educational roles of the public schools before successful plans of school restructuring can be developed.**

Although the role of schools varies from community to community, increasingly, almost all school districts are being required to help fill the gap in public and private services. Schools are being asked to provide such social and developmental programs as health care and child care, drug education, AIDS education, services for teenage parents and dropouts, suicide prevention, and mentoring, among others.

A study conducted by the Minnesota Business Partnership found that the most common complaint among school superintendents, both urban and rural, was a continuing increase in legislative mandates and interference with the operations of the school system. Such mandates, which usually focus on inputs rather than on results, are often made without the means to carry them out, placing huge burdens on the schools and depleting their resources. The entire program, both academic and social, suffers as a result.[1]

ELEMENTS OF RESTRUCTURING

The restructuring of education has taken different routes in different communities. Only a few school systems have as yet undertaken a top-to-bottom overhaul, but some of these restructuring efforts have been in place long enough to provide important lessons on how this can be done at the state, district, and local school levels. The key elements needed for successful restructuring of education include: a communitywide commitment to change; performance-based goals; incentives and accountability for performance, such as a greater role for teachers in decision making; better ways of assessing results; more positive attitudes among parents and students; and resources that match the school system's needs.

COMMITMENT TO CHANGE

The most important criteria for creating and institutionalizing change, whether it is in a school building, a school district, or the broad system of human investment, is a communitywide consensus and commitment. A Rand Corporation study of reform efforts in six cities concluded that two key elements must be present in order to sustain broad public support for change: First, there must be public support for reform based on the understanding that the failure of the education system could threaten the social and economic future of the community, rather than on the promise of a quick fix. If this recognition of the importance of the problem is present, the Rand Study concluded, support can be sustained through the long process of trial and error that communities must undergo to improve schooling. Second, there must be the active involvement and support of a coalition of community leaders, most importantly the business community, local political leaders, the teachers union, and the school superintendent.[2] Business leaders have three roles to play: first, providing the broad strategic thinking that places educational problems in the context of other community economic and social issues; second, providing funds to underwrite initiatives; and third and most important, putting educational problems at the top of the local agenda.

In a number of states and communities, such as South Carolina, Kentucky, Rochester (New York), and Miami, where this broad public and business commitment has become a regular part of the educational landscape, meaningful structural change in education is taking root. Even in communities such as Boston, where improvements in educational outcomes have not been as readily achievable as initially expected, the commitment of business leaders has not flagged. If anything, initial disappointment in the ability of the Boston Compact to lower the dropout rate and improve the overall achievement of students has led the business community to take a more militant stance in favor of more structural change in education, including implementing school-based management and a public school choice plan.

The development, promotion, and implementation of South Carolina's Education Improvement Act (EIA) provides an instructive example of how constituencies for reform can be built and maintained. As far back as 1983, South Carolina received national attention for passing one of the most comprehensive state reform packages in the nation. In 1989, the state piggybacked a second reform bill, called Target 2000. In both pieces of legislation, South Carolina's business community played a crucial role in setting the agenda for reform and getting legislation passed (see page 42).

PERFORMANCE-BASED GOALS

The only true measure of school success is what graduates know and can do when they complete their education. In earlier decades, when the high school diploma was a meaningful measure of academic achievement, employers could hire high school graduates with confidence. As the schools experienced dramatic changes in student population and social

BUSINESS INVOLVEMENT IN SOUTH CAROLINA'S EDUCATION REFORM PROGRAM

Business involvement was critical to South Carolina's passage of two major statewide reform initiatives. Some of the key provisions of the second education improvement act, called Target 2000, included:

- Incentives for encouraging school-site restructuring.
- School-based programs for four-year-old at-risk children that are now mandatory in every district.
- Grants for school-based parenting education for parents of children from birth to age five.
- Expanding compensatory education programs to bring students up to grade level using demonstration grants for model and pilot projects designed to reduce school dropout rates.
- Encouraging districts to go beyond teaching basic skills to developing curricula and evaluation procedures for teaching higher-order skills.
- Expanding school accountability.
- The creation of a new advisory committee by state legislation, made up of thirty-two prominent business, civic, government, and education leaders to advise the state on education policy issues.

Business support was crucial for passage of both reform efforts and for their continued promotion, assessment, and reevaluation. It is instructive to take a look at the strategy used by the state to develop and maintain the support of business, the public, and the press. There were five key steps.

- Extensive polling to gauge community interest in education reform.
- Recruiting of top corporate executives to help develop the reform package.
- Promotion of the reform package through a comprehensive information and advertising campaign.
- Invitations to both business and the press to visit schools.
- Ongoing communication with the public on the progress of reform.

SOURCE: Business Advisory Committee of the South Carolina Education Improvement Act.

climate, the measure of success shifted from what students knew and could do at the end of twelve years of education to the number of years students were retained in school. Confidence in the high school diploma has declined to such a low level that many employers will no longer hire graduates directly out of high school, insisting instead that entry-level workers have at least some college education.

In business, success is determined primarily by how well a product sells in the marketplace. Establishing performance goals to measure how well the company's products are doing is one of the basic require-ments for staying competitive. No company would expect to stay in business for long without setting targets for production, sales, and profits and readjusting business strategies when achievement falls short of preestablished bench-marks.

Similarly, no reform or restructuring program for education can be successful unless there is communitywide agreement on the goals of education. This is the only way to ensure that restructuring strategies are having their desired effect and to avoid disappointment and disillusion-ment with the reform process when achievement falls short of the mark. Furthermore, unless the education system has clearer goals and more effective methods of measurement, it cannot be more accountable for results. **We urge business to take leadership in their communities and work with educators, public officials, and other segments of the commu-nity to develop goals for education and measures of performance that reflect the real skills and knowledge students will need when they embark on their adult responsibilities.**

Important progress is being made at the national, state, and local levels to better define what the results of education should be. The President and the nation's governors have provided critically needed national leadership by developing and mutually endorsing a broad-based set of six national goals for education to be achieved by the year 2000.

- All children will start school ready to learn.

- The high school graduation rate will be at least 90 percent.

- Students will leave grades four, eight, and twelve having demon-strated competency over challenging subject matter, and all students will be prepared for responsible citizenship, future learning, and productive employment.

- U.S. students will be first in the world in math and science.

- All American adults will be literate, able to compete in a global economy, and able to exercise responsible citizenship.

- Every school will have an environment conducive to learning and free of drugs and violence.

Although the national goals at first seemed overly ambitious, they have represented a critical first step toward more accurately defining what the nation should expect from its education system. At its meeting in July 1990, the National Governors' Association, in collaboration with the Administration, identified key strategies for achieving these goals. They ranged from ensuring access to prenatal and well-child care to help achieve the goal of readiness to designing incentive programs to achieve the goal of increased high school graduation rates.

The national goals initiative provides important national leadership for ensuring that all children are educated well; yet, it is only a first step. The larger task remains ahead. Public education is still primarily a state and local responsibility, and there is considerable variation from community to community in the quality of the schools, the needs of students, and the resources available. Specific goals for educational attainment and strategies for meeting those goals should be developed at the state level, in local school districts, and for each school. Goals should also involve other institutions that have responsibility for child development and that affect children's readiness for school. At the same time, the states should provide guidance and resources to help local districts and schools meet their goals, and local schools and school districts should be given wider latitude in deciding how to deploy available educational resources most effectively.

We believe that every state and local community should take an inventory of its schools and the related community institutions that have an impact on the health, development, and education of its children. This effort should involve a representative cross-section of the community, including business, parents, teachers, administrators, government officials, and civic leaders, to identify goals for students and the system, strategies for attaining those goals, and appropriate accountability measures to assess whether the goals are being reached within a reasonable time frame.

A number of important efforts in this direction are currently under way. The Council of Great City Schools, which represents the forty-seven largest school systems in the nation, and its Task Force on Goals, chaired by New York City Schools Chancellor Joseph Fernandez, has developed a set of education goals patterned on the national goals but designed to address the specific needs and problems of urban school systems. The urban education task force also enlisted the help of leaders in education, government, business, and the community to develop specific strategies for meeting each of the goals. The National Assessment of Educational Progress (NAEP) will be developing new performance standards that will

EDUCATION REFORM IN OHIO

At the urging of Governor Richard Celeste, in June 1989, the Ohio General Assembly passed the Education Improvement Program, which incorporates most of the recommendations proposed by the Ohio Citizen's Commission on the Year 2000, chaired by Owen B. Butler, retired chairman of The Procter & Gamble Company and chairman of CED.

The legislation established an executive and legislative Commission on Education Improvement to monitor results and an Education Improvement Fund to expand existing programs and support new programs to address dropout rates, teen pregnancy, and the needs of at-risk children. Included for the first time was state-subsidized preschool, making Ohio only the ninth state to provide significant financial support for Head Start. Other aspects of the Education Improvement Program include:

Student testing and reporting of results. Results of required student testing in grades four, six, eight, and ten will be reported to the state by school and by grade and will be entered into a newly established management information system. Systemwide performance goals will be set for preschool through high school education. The system will monitor data on student participation and performance, employees, and cost accounting.

Open enrollment. By July 1993, all school districts must adopt policies permitting open-enrollment within their district boundaries. Districts may also permit open enrollment with adjacent districts with the understanding that the funding for a student will go to the district in which he is enrolled, not where he resides.

Deregulation. Those schools identified as excellent may request an exemption from state rules or statutes. The state board of education may grant such exemptions for up to five years. Also, a school may request deregulation in order to implement an "innovative education pilot program."

SOURCE: Office of the Governor Richard F. Celeste

define for the first time what students in grades four, eight, and twelve should know and be able to do. At the federal level, both the Department of Labor and the Department of Energy have undertaken similar projects. The Department of Labor's Commission on Achieving Necessary Skills is attempting to better define the skill requirements of a broad range of jobs expected to be growth occupations in the future, and the Department of Energy will be examining new strategies for improving achievement in math and science.

A number of business organizations are also directly involved in supporting the need for clearer educational goals. The Business Roundtable has established a ten-year project to work with governors and other leaders at the state level to identify, set, and implement education goals. The U.S. Chamber of Commerce has recently launched a new effort to assist its 3,000 local chambers in working on education reform at the local level, with implementation of education goals as a major focus. And the American Business Conference has developed a new initiative, Vital Link, which is an innovative program to encourage students not planning to attend college to work toward their full potential and understand the employment and training options available to them.

Some states have already made progress in addressing the need for performance-based goals. As the result of recommendations made in 1989 by a statewide citizens' commission, Ohio is currently in the process of creating an education system that focuses on results. Performance goals are being set for preschool through high school education, and an executive and legislative Commission on Education Improvement has been created to monitor the results of reform efforts (see page 45).

In Seattle, a citywide Education Summit resulted in a strategic plan to implement a broad set of goals. These include making schools the focal point of the community, celebrating cultural diversity in the schools, making sure every child is safe, healthy, and ready to learn, enhancing the learning environment for students and teachers, and enhancing education funding. The Summit Implementation Group represents a broad cross-section of the community, including the Mayor's Office, the City Council, the Seattle School Board, the Greater Seattle Chamber of Commerce, United Way, the Seattle Public Schools, parent, teacher, and principals organizations, higher education, and many others.

INCENTIVES AND ACCOUNTABILITY

Neither people nor institutions are inclined to change unless there is a compelling reason to do so. In business, people are induced to work harder if they are offered incentives such as better working conditions, more autonomy, the promise of a promotion, or higher pay or bonuses in exchange for better results. Disincentives in the form of sanctions can also motivate changes in performance. For example, the fear of being fired or demoted can be a spur to better performance.

In public education, there are few incentives that motivate people to do a better job. It is not only teachers and administrators who fail to see the benefits of change; most students have very little incentive to work harder and learn more.

School systems at the state and local levels are beginning to apply a number of strategies to help change the incentive structure in education. Chief among these is introducing greater competition into education through public school choice. Another strategy, which stresses sanctions over positive incentives, is educational bankruptcy, in which the state education department or district central office will shut down and reorganize schools that clearly are not working. A more positive incentive mechanism is affording school systems that work greater flexibility in organization and design and a measure of freedom from restrictive regulatory control at the state or district level. School-based management, which has become one of the principal elements in most districtwide restructuring initiatives, is based on the notion that flexibility and accountability at the local school level will enable school personnel to employ the strategies that best meet the diverse learning needs of their students. However, few school reform strategies have emphasized the importance of providing incentives to students that will encourage them to work harder, learn better, and take greater responsibility for becoming educated.

PUBLIC SCHOOL CHOICE. One of the most controversial issues of the current restructuring debate is the expansion of school choice. At least twenty states and a significant number of municipalities have made school choice a key strategy for educational improvement, and many more are considering it.

School choice has two main purposes: The first is to give all parents, rich and poor alike, greater discretion in choosing public schools that best meet their children's needs. The second is to give schools the incentive to improve their educational offerings by requiring them to compete for students.**

There are generally two types of choice plans. The first, which is employed in most states and districts that allow choice, is a system open only to public schools. These plans can involve a single district, cross district lines within a region, or involve all districts in the state. Many are based on the creation of magnet schools, which offer special programs to attract students throughout a district or a group of neighboring districts.

---

*See memoranda by JAMES Q. RIORDAN (page 92).

---

*See memoranda by HENRY SCHACHT (page 93).

**See memoranda by HENRY SCHACHT (page 93).

The second allows students to choose either public or private schools, providing a set amount of tuition in the form of a voucher equivalent to the per pupil expenditure in a state or district. The most visible experiment with this kind of voucher system has taken place in Milwaukee, which in the 1990-91 school year has provided the opportunity for up to 1,000 low-income students (out of 98,000 students systemwide) to choose to attend any school, public or private, at public expense. Initially, only 400 students took advantage of the voucher system. Although the Milwaukee program was recently struck down by the state court on a technicality, there is support at the state level for reimplementing and expanding the program.

The concept of choice is deceptively simple on the surface and appealing in a society based on a free-market economy, but the implications for public schools are remarkably complex. It is assumed that choice will impel public schools to behave more like businesses, which try to attract new customers by offering better products or products that fill specific consumer needs. Theoretically, this would result in good schools attracting more students and expanding, with bad schools losing students and being forced to improve their offerings or go out of business. In practice, the results of choice are unlikely to be so clear-cut. Although losing pupils might actually make it easier for a less successful school to serve those who remain behind, a more successful school would have little incentive for attracting additional pupils if it had no place for them or if it had to accommodate larger class sizes. This could pose a particular problem in choice plans where students are allowed to cross district lines. In Minnesota's plan, for example, children who cross district lines bring with them only their state per pupil allocation, which amounts to about 70 percent of the total per pupil cost. Having to make up the additional 30 percent cost per student would provide little encouragement for a district to accept outsiders.

An even more critical issue is how to ensure that all children, especially the most disadvantaged, receive a quality education. These are the children who would be most likely to remain in the worst-performing schools because their parents are unable or unwilling to act as their advocates. It might take several years for central school authorities to determine that a school was unable to improve its performance, and by then the damage to students would already have been done.

New research into student achievement demonstrates that, by itself, choice does not guarantee educational quality.[3] Instead, choice often becomes an easy political solution to a tough educational problem. Where the quality of education is generally high and all children can find a school that matches their learning styles and needs, choice makes sense. *In Investing in Our Children*, CED proposed the development of a "universal magnet school plan" in which every public school in a jurisdiction would offer special programs and be open to every student in the area.[3]

We believe that where choice systems are put into place, they should involve the public schools only.* The public schools are vital for preserving the democratic principles that promote good citizenship and common values. Furthermore, the first obligation of society is to guarantee a quality education to all children, not just to the lucky few who happen to live in the right neighborhood or who have parents who can work the system on their behalf. It is precisely the most vulnerable children who may be left behind in a market-driven choice system. Where choice has been in place for a considerable period of time, as it has in New York City's District 4, located in East Harlem, its actual impact on student achievement has been mixed (see page 50).**

In some segments of higher education, where choice has long shaped educational offerings, the free market has sometimes been subject to abuse. An example is the nation's system of trade schools, which were developed to provide postsecondary vocational and professional training for students who do not go on to college. A 1984 survey of proprietary trade schools found that half admitted students who did not meet federally mandated admission requirements. Of these students, 74 percent dropped out without having gotten the training they expected, and two-thirds of these schools misrepresented themselves in recruiting students by lying about the job prospects of graduates.[5] ***

Taking these concerns into account, we support the implementation of public school choice where it is part of an overall plan to restructure the schools, where accountability measures are clearly laid out, and where the special needs of the disadvantaged are taken into account. Under these circumstances, school choice can inject a refreshing note of diversity into education, provide incentives for all schools to strive for excellence, and help families find the schools that best meet their children's learning styles and educational needs. The following criteria developed for Minnesota's school choice plan offer useful guidelines for choice programs in general:

- There should be a list of academic and other performance goals that all schools must include in their programs.

- The plan should provide assistance for parents in selecting among various programs for their children.

- Entrance requirements should promote racial integration and must

---

*See memoranda by GEORGE C. EADS (page 93).

**See memoranda by HENRY SCHACHT (page 93).

***See memoranda by HENRY SCHACHT (page 94).

not discriminate against students on the basis of past achievement or behavior.

- All schools within a specific geographic area must be given encouragement and assistance to develop distinctive features, rather than allowing resources to be concentrated at a few magnet schools in that district.

- There must be opportunities for teachers and principals to help create distinctive, quality programs.

- Transportation must be provided within a reasonable area for all students.

- Continuing oversight and modification must be a part of the plan.

PUBLIC SCHOOL CHOICE IN EAST HARLEM

One of the best-known choice programs operates in New York City's District 4, located in the inner-city community of East Harlem. The District 4 program began in 1974 with the creation of a series of small magnet schools, mostly developed by teachers, with each focusing on a different program or area of concentration.

The choice system was not introduced until the early 1980s, when nearly all the district's junior high schools housed these alternative programs and prospective junior high school students were required to select their schools. The magnet programs are also highly successful in attracting middle-class students from outside the district.

Overall reading scores have improved considerably since 1972, when only 15 percent of the district's students read at grade level, the lowest in the city. By 1989, 48 percent were at grade level or above, placing the district about midway among the city's thirty-two local school districts.

Some critics contend that some of this increase is attributable to outside students who attend the magnet programs, and others say that the students most at risk rarely get accepted to the best programs in the district. In addition, the alternative schools do not operate on the same budgets as the regular schools in the district. They receive extra funding through the federal Magnet Schools Assistance Grants program, which allows them to hire more teachers, reduce class size, and provide materials and equipment to develop thematic programs.

SOURCE: *Education Week*, "Known for Choice, New York's District 4 Offers a Complex Tale for Urban Reformers," November 1, 1989.

RELIEVING THE REGULATORY BURDEN ON QUALITY SCHOOLS. Although the federal government contributes only 6 percent of total federal funds to education, mostly through programs such as Head Start, Chapter 1, vocational education, education for the handicapped, the Magnet Schools Assistance Grants, and a variety of other programs, the use of these funds by state and local governments is sometimes overly constrained by burdensome and often conflicting federal regulations. This often prevents the deployment of more rational and cost-effective problem-solving strategies, such as the integration and coordination of programs that address similar needs and target populations. One of the key outcomes of the National Education Summit was recognition of the need for greater flexibility and coordination among education programs and a pledge by the federal government to lower the regulatory burden on states and localities in exchange for a higher level of accountability.

We fully support greater flexibility in the use of federal funds for education and child development programs and better coordination of programs at the state and local level. However, greater flexibility should be contingent on increased accountability to ensure that funds are being used to achieve results that were originally intended.

SCHOOL-BASED MANAGEMENT. We continue our long support for bottom-up reform strategies that focus change as close to the point of learning as possible: the school building, the classroom, and the interaction between teacher and student. The movement toward affording schools greater autonomy and flexibility in how they carry out their educational mission is taking hold in school systems around the country and having tangible effects on the achievement of students, their attitude toward school, and the professionalism and collegiality of teachers and administrative staff.

Various forms of school-site management were pioneered in Miami-Dade County and Rochester as part of historic contract agreements made between the school system and the teachers union in each of those locations. Even earlier, an effective school-based management program was created and first implemented in New Haven by Dr. James P. Comer, a child psychiatrist who designed a system of school improvement that provided not only teachers but also parents with a role in the management of schools.

The purpose of school-site management is to offer teachers, other school personnel, and increasingly, parents a greater say in the decision-making process in their school. Other cities now implementing forms of school-based management include New York City (whose chancellor, Joseph Fernandez, helped develop the school-based management program in Miami), Los Angeles, Boston, and Chicago.

School-based management provides the opportunity for teachers and other school personnel to address the particular educational needs and problems of their students in a creative way. One approach that is gaining in popularity is assigning groups of students to a team of teachers

---

EDUCATION RESTRUCTURING IN MIAMI

Approximately half of Miami-Dade County's 260 schools have converted to the innovative education system of school-based management/shared decision making (SBM/SDM). In these schools, classroom teachers enjoy direct participation in decision making. A "cabinet" of teachers, administrators, and the principal share the power to determine personnel, school design, class size, curriculum, budget, and other matters. Hand in hand with this new responsibility are teacher contracts that provide for competitive teacher salaries (the average salary is $39,646; the highest is $64,000), making Dade's teachers among the best paid in the nation.

In addition to the new role of teachers, Dade County's public schools feature several other innovations. Highlights include:

Leadership Experience Opportunities (LEO). This career ladders program offers eighteen weeks of on-site administrative experiences to teachers interested in becoming assistant principals and eventually principals.

Summer School. Dade Country has the largest summer school program in the nation. Summer school provides students with opportunities to accelerate their academic progress. Sixty-one percent of Dade's students attended summer school in 1989.

Saturday Morning School. More than 60 schools hold classes on Saturday mornings in an effort to improve performance of students considered at risk of dropping out. Students voluntarily attend classes in reading, writing, and arithmetic.

Child Care. Dade County public schools offer one of the largest child care programs in the country. Some 12,000 elementary school youngsters enjoy supervised after-school child care until 6:00 p.m.; another 1,000 students are enrolled in before-school care.

Dade Academy for Teaching Arts (DATA). These nine-week minisabbaticals allow teachers to pursue creative and innovative projects and engage in educational research.

SOURCE: Dade County Public Schools.

over a period of several years in order to provide continuity in learning, reduce student anonymity, and increase accountability for performance. This approach, which has been used successfully in some West German schools for the past 20 years, is now being adapted in a number of U.S. schools. An early American pioneer using this approach is D. W. Griffith Junior High in East Los Angeles (see page 54).

ASSESSING ACHIEVEMENT*

Without meaningful methods of assessing student achievement, it will be very difficult to gauge the progress of education reforms or sustain the long-term commitment of business and the public. A major new study by the National Commission on Testing and Public Policy confirms the inadequacy of current testing mechanisms, which rely almost exclusively on multiple-choice examination. The study found that most tests currently in use are misleading indicators of student performance, that schools test too much and consume too many school days to prepare for tests, and that the fixation on test results deflects attention from fundamental educational problems. Nevertheless, the Commission found that there is no single existing form of testing or assessment that is universally better than group-administered multiple-choice tests, which provide useful information. Rather, the Commission recommended the use of a variety of assessment tools to provide more accurate judgments of individuals, groups, and institutions and a better basis for educational decision making.[6]

New assessment mechanisms are needed that not only measure the facts students have learned but also more accurately assess what students can do with the knowledge they have acquired. Several promising initiatives currently under way seek to revolutionize the way student achievement and, by inference, school productivity are assessed. In New York State, the state superintendent recently called for the development of a portfolio assessment system for all students. Such a system would require teachers to evaluate students on the basis of a portfolio of work that the student would build during the school year. The assignments given to students to build their portfolios would presumably include a majority of written work in the form of essays and papers that would present a better analysis of their ability to apply what they are learning using skills that will be required of them in later life.

A more far-reaching initiative to develop a more accurate inventory of basic and higher-order skills and knowledge that students need at various stages in their academic careers is being spearheaded by the National Assessment of Educational Progress (NAEP).

---

*See memoranda by DONALD M. STEWART (page 94).

LOS ANGELES SCHOOL EXPERIMENT

A group of Los Angeles teachers of predominantly Hispanic students have adopted a highly regarded organizational model known as the *team/small group model,* used in a number of West German Schools for the past twenty years.

The formula is simple: Teachers are divided into small, relatively autonomous teams, with each team responsible for one group of students. The teams stay with their students from the fifth grade until precollegiate education ends in the tenth grade. Time is set aside during the school week for the members of each team to meet with one another to plan how they will go about teaching the state-mandated curriculum.

Most classwork takes place in small table groups made up of four to six students of varying academic abilities and social backgrounds. Students typically stay with their table group throughout the six grades.

This model fosters close personal relationships between teachers and students and provides the teachers with the opportunity to interact professionally on a daily basis with their team members. In the German school where this concept was first developed, the dropout rate is only 1 percent, compared with 14 percent overall in Germany. Sixty percent of the students test well enough on the country's rigorous high school exit exams to be admitted to a four-year college.

The first American school where this concept is being tried is D. W. Griffith Junior High in East Los Angeles, where virtually all students are poor enough to qualify for reduced-price lunches. The teaching team will stay with their students for their three years in junior high and have decided to abolish letter grades, evaluating students instead on individual skills.

The first year of the program required major adjustments by both teachers and students, and several students who could not adjust left the group. Now, in the program's second year, the teachers note a number of successes. Student discipline has improved, students realize they cannot be anonymous and slide by without doing work, and they have grown more comfortable with school. For teachers, the major benefits have been increased collegiality, the opportunity to get to know students better, and an end to the isolation experienced by most teachers in traditional classrooms.

Schools in San Francisco, Toledo, and at least four other locations are beginning to experiment with this approach.

SOURCE: *Education Week,* November 1, 1989.

ROLE OF PARENTS AND STUDENTS

THE CURRICULUM OF THE HOME. Numerous studies have shown that the attitudes and values of children and teenagers are shaped more by their parents than by any other factor, including school and peers. Similarly, family life has a critical impact on educational achievement. A study by the National Governors' Association found that a negative *home curriculum* accounts for half the problems students can have in school, and a recent study of achievement patterns in New Jersey's schools found that students' backgrounds accounted for most of the achievement differentials from one district to the other.[7] Parents are their children's first and most important teachers, a responsibility that does not end when children enter school.

Children learn through a variety of means. The schools are generally expected to teach a knowledge-based curriculum that includes such subjects as reading, writing, mathematics, science, history, and foreign languages. This is the subject matter, which constitutes the *visible curriculum.* Over the years educators and society at large have determined that this curriculum provides the knowledge necessary to enable children to develop into productive adults and responsible citizens.[8]

But long before children enter school and are exposed to this knowledge-based curriculum, they are learning lessons that are likely to have a greater long-term impact on their ability to function successfully as adults, whether in the workplace, as citizens, or in their relationships with others in their families, with their peers, and in their community. These lessons are learned through the *invisible curriculum* that pervades the home, the community, the media, and the education system.

The invisible curriculum consists of all the messages that adults send to children about what is valued and respected in the adult world. These messages are critical for shaping the character of children, their outlook on life, and their ability to interact effectively with others. The content of the invisible curriculum helps teach children how much value to place on themselves and others. It develops and reinforces good habits, shared values, and high standards of behavior, all of which are likely to produce adults who succeed in education and in life.

An effective invisible curriculum stresses, among other things, good work habits, teamwork, perseverance, honesty, self-reliance, and consideration for others. These "character builders" are as important to future success in the workplace and in life as the academic skills taught through the regular curriculum and should be stressed in the home as well as in the school. Just as every school should pay particular attention to the content of its invisible curriculum, parents need to reinforce the positive values that will help their children become better and more responsible learners.

Now that the majority of children live with either a single parent or two parents who work full time, families need more help from schools and employers to enable them to focus on their children's education. Schools should increase direct communication with parents and find more ways to involve parents in their children's schooling. One of the most successful projects to improve the commitment of inner-city parents to their children's education is the school-based management process first instituted over twenty years ago in New Haven's schools by James P. Comer. On the preschool level, programs that directly involve parents in the development and education of their children, such as Parents as Teachers and the Kenan Family Literacy Program, have shown remarkable long-term results.

Parents also need help from employers. Employers should be willing to implement workplace policies that reflect their concern with education and provide parents with the time and support they need in order to be more involved and take greater responsibility for their children's education. Strategies such as release time or flexible scheduling would allow parents who are hourly workers to take part in school activities or hold conferences with teachers.

STUDENT RESPONSIBILITY. In placing the blame for our educational decline at the doorstep of the school or in the lap of parents, many policy makers have forgotten that learning is not a passive experience. Only someone who is actively engaged in the learning process will become an educated person. Few reform strategies have acknowledged the fundamental importance of asking students to take responsibility for their own education.

Instead, most educational models describe students as either *products* or *consumers*. The traditional model of education views students as the end products of educational factories, whose purpose is to turn out graduates who know and can do something useful for society. A second model casts students as consumers of education. In this view, the students have the power to accept or reject the education they are offered.

We believe that both approaches incorrectly view students as the passive recipients of education. Rather, we believe that students will become truly educated only if they are encouraged to take greater control of their educational experiences and opportunities. Students are the *workers* of education; they can enhance their own personal capital by learning more and learning better. In this way they are likely to become more desirable to employers and better prepared to assume the responsibilities of civic life. In this view, teachers and administrators play a different role as well. They must become the *managers* of the education process, whose job it is to guide students in their work, provide incentives for them to work harder, and enable them to do the best possible job.

Unfortunately, public education currently provides very few incentives for students to work hard at getting higher grades or to take demanding courses unless they are among the small minority who are bound for a selective college. Most graduates will qualify for some college, somewhere; and for the 50 percent headed directly into the work force, the incentives for working hard while in high school are even fewer. Few employers who hire entry-level workers directly out of high school ask about grades or courses taken. Proof of graduation is generally adequate, and testing helps screen out those without the literacy or numeracy skills required by the job.

Both schools and business should do more to encourage students to see learning as preparation for adult work. **We recommend that employers, with the support of schools, ask prospective entry-level employees for high school transcripts or report cards.** This would provide an increased incentive for students to make better decisions about their future while still in school. The Educational Testing Service is in the process of developing a national resume bank that would assist students in building a personal file to provide prospective employers. It would include their grades, a history of the coursework they have taken, and any relevant work or volunteer experience they have engaged in during and immediately after high school.

MENTORING FOR AT-RISK CHILDREN AND YOUTH. Not all families can provide the support and caring needed for student success in school or in life. Many children are disadvantaged precisely because their parents are unable or unwilling to provide the positive role models all children need. In some cases, even when parents have the best intentions, they have few resources for introducing their children to experiences that go beyond the neighborhood, broaden their horizons, and help them negotiate an unfamiliar world. This is particularly true for minority males in the inner city, for whom successful role models are often absent.

An important response to this problem has been the development of formal mentoring programs that match a young person with an adult in a mutually enriching relationship. Mentoring is becoming a significant component of business-school partnership programs. Support of mentoring programs lends itself well to corporate objectives of better utilizing human resources by promoting employee involvement and volunteer efforts in the community. Some mentoring programs focus primarily on career objectives by matching students with successful individuals in professional or crafts fields, such as the Mentor in Law and Mentor in Advertising programs run by the New York Alliance for the Public Schools in New York City. General Electric counts on its employees to help reach the company's goal of doubling the number of college-bound youths in selected poor and inner-city schools. GE's employees serve as mentors and tutors in the College Bound Program, which also provides support for selected districts to develop locally designed curricula in addition to mentors and tutors for youth. Mutual Of New York's mentoring program pairs employees in one-to-one tutoring relationships with fifth graders at the Kennedy Magnet School in the Port Chester, New York, school district. The program's goals are both to improve the reading skills of students and to help them learn to love reading.

In many business-school partnerships where mentoring is not the primary focus, it is often a critical element for success. For example, the "I Have A Dream" program, which provides scholarship money to encourage children to complete high school and go on to college, considers mentoring crucial. Founder Eugene Lang established a guidance and support mechanism for the students participating in the program and has frequently stated that it would not have succeeded without the personal involvement of the program sponsor and trained adult mentors. Some of the public programs based on the "I Have a Dream" model, such as New York State's Liberty Scholarship Program, are incorporating mentoring and guidance into the program design in recognition of their importance in keeping teenagers in school.

Mentoring programs should also carefully consider the feelings of the parents of participating children. Mentors should not try to assume parental authority or contradict parental values. Parents should not be made to feel that they are inferior to the mentor either in values or in material wealth.

Mentoring programs can offer valuable rewards for disadvantaged youth and for participating adults. Intensive personal relationships with adults are for the most part absent from the usual societal assistance programs for youths. The experience of young people suggests that mentoring can help fill that gap, and the resulting intergenerational bonds may impart essential skills for surviving in a tumultuous world where developing psychological and social maturity may be just as crucial to achieving long-term self-sufficiency as a firm grip on the three Rs.

Volunteers are critical to the success of mentoring and other programs, such as preschool, that call for increased interaction between adults and children. **We urge business to encourage employees and other adults to volunteer in a variety of education and child development programs.** Business should also provide the training and supervision necessary to ensure a successful volunteer experience.

TECHNOLOGICAL INNOVATION IN EDUCATION

The more widespread application of advanced technologies to education is an area of untapped potential for increasing the productivity of teachers and addressing the individual learning needs of students. Although technology has drastically improved most other major aspects of human endeavor, including scientific research and development, medicine, communications, transportation, government, defense, energy, business, entertainment, housekeeping, and food preparation, relatively little has been done to expand its use in education, particularly in schools that serve disadvantaged students.

Technology-based learning refers to instructional materials and techniques that use the organization, storage, retrieval, and communication capabilities of technology to provide learners with instructional materials that match their preparation level, learning style, interest areas, learning pace, and desired learning location. Computers can free teachers from boring drill and practice sessions and make learning more enjoyable for the students by providing individualized instruction, more time on the task, and a nonjudgmental environment. In addition, sophisticated computer-based interactive programs are very good at teaching reasoning, logic, and problem solving.

IBM's Writing to Read is one of the best known and most widely used computer-based education programs that focuses on developing the writing and reading skills of children in preschool and the elementary grades. Recently, IBM designated $25 million to increase innovative use of computers in the classroom.

A number of states are actively pursuing the introduction of advanced learning technologies into the classroom. In Texas, the state board of education recently voted to allow school districts to buy a videodisk-based science curriculum with state textbook funds, a move that is likely to encourage traditional publishers to step up their efforts to produce electronic learning materials. In addition, the Texas board had previously voted to open all future textbook adoptions to electronic publishers.

The Mississippi 2000 project, a collaboration among BellSouth's subsidiary South Central Bell, Northern Telecom, and the state government, will enable four rural high schools to become part of an innovative fiber optic network that will supplement local classes through interactive televised instruction. Mississippi 2000 will serve as a model to demonstrate the use of fiber optics for long-distance learning that can be replicated in other areas of Mississippi and BellSouth's nine-state region.

The state will provide each school with an electronic classroom equipped with transmitting and receiving equipment and personal computers for multimedia presentations. Teachers in each of the four schools will interact with teachers at Mississippi State University, Mississippi University for Women, and Mississippi Educational Television, and some instruction will originate from the Mississippi School for Mathematics and Science. Classes can originate from and be received by any of the sites; and in addition to seeing and hearing the teacher, students in any location can gain immediate on-camera access and ask questions or make comments.

EDUCATIONAL RESOURCES

Quality education is not an expense, but an investment in the future of the nation. What the nation spends to improve the health, development, and education of its children will be returned many times over in increased productivity and competitiveness and lowered costs of welfare, crime, and social unrest.

Investing in quality education and child development means that we will have to place our resources where they are needed most. In some cases, this can be accomplished with few additional funds. For example, implementing a school-based management program requires important changes in attitude and lines of authority but few new financial resources. On the other hand, increasing the salaries of teachers and child care professionals, improving the physical plant of many badly deteriorated inner-city schools, and providing new technology and upgrading text-books will undoubtedly require an infusion of new capital. So, too, will such key preventive measures as expanding the availability and access of poor families to prenatal care, child care, and preschool education. But streamlining service delivery through interagency coordination and case management may also help save money in the long term.

As a society, we cannot afford to ignore or postpone improvements in our schools or in child development because our future is at risk. In *Children in Need,* we stated that "any plan for major improvements in the development and education of disadvantaged children that does not recognize the need for additional resources over a sustained period is doomed to failure." Nevertheless, where additional resources are not immediately forthcoming, wiser allocation of existing resources must be a primary objective of reform efforts.

EQUITABLE FUNDING OF SCHOOLS. Although funding for education increased substantially during the 1980s, education spending actually declined slightly as a proportion of the gross national product to just over 3.5 percent. Nevertheless, in real terms, overall state and local spending rose 26 percent between 1980 and 1988. This increase varied substantially from region to region. In the Middle West, school funds rose only 11 percent; in the Southeast, they rose 34 percent; and in the Far West, they rose 49 percent.[9] The federal share has actually declined by 2 percent in real terms while local expenditures have increased 15 percent. Almost all local education revenues are still produced by property taxes. This can result in major differences. Although poorer districts tax property at a higher rate, the lower tax base usually yields fewer dollars overall and per pupil allocations that can be several thousand dollars lower than in wealthier districts. The gap between rich and poor districts is over $2,000 per pupil in California, over $6,500 in New York, and over $8,000 in Ohio.

These disparities in local funding are fueling a growing nationwide movement to revamp state education funding mechanisms in order to guarantee more equitable funding of rich and poor school districts. A number of recent state supreme court decisions have declared funding mechanisms used to finance education to be unconstitutional. In the past eighteen months alone, courts have struck down the financing systems of New Jersey, Texas, and Montana. Similar cases are pending in a dozen other states, including Alaska, and Connecticut. Some states, such as Kentucky and Oklahoma, in order to avoid having decisions about their financing systems made in the courts, have taken the initiative to redesign their funding systems and make them part of a statewide school-restructuring program. New Jersey recently voted to phase out millions of dollars in state aid now received by the 150 most affluent districts and to increase state support for poor cities and moderate-income suburbs.

We applaud this movement toward more equitable allocation of resources among school districts. Nevertheless, we do not believe that wealthier districts should be constrained from contributing what they believe to be an appropriate level of resources to educate their children. We believe that states should be responsible for seeing to it that all local systems have sufficient resources to ensure the essential elements of a satisfactory school program. However, state financing formulas should also provide local communities with the authority and the incentives to raise and allocate funds at the local level.

HUMAN RESOURCES: A CHANGING TEACHER WORK FORCE

Schools can be no better than the teachers who staff them. Our success in restructuring the nation's schools will depend largely on our ability to attract highly qualified people to the profession of teaching, keep them in it, and improve their overall effectiveness.

Impending changes in the demographics of teaching pose both a challenge and an opportunity. In 1988, there were approximately 2.6 million teachers working in both public and private schools. By 1992, roughly 1.3 million new teachers will be hired, an amount equivalent to half of all teachers currently working. It is estimated that it would require 23 percent of each college graduating class to meet the projected need for teachers through the early 1990s. Despite a recent increase of 61 percent in the number of young people considering entering the profession, only about 9 percent of entering freshmen indicate teaching as a career aspiration. And there is as yet no indication that the poor quality of the average teacher candidate has improved appreciably in the past few years. We are particularly concerned about the widening gap between a growing minority student population and a decreasing number of minority teachers.

These trends suggest two responses. One is to find ways to improve the quality of the teaching profession by attracting more qualified candidates, improving the education and training of prospective teachers, and improving and enhancing the skills of those now in the classroom. The second is to develop new roles for teachers and to reorganize the process of teaching so that experienced teachers can become managers of the educational process.

In *Investing in Our Children,* CED called for "nothing less than a revolution in the role of the teacher and the management of the schools." It is encouraging that this revolution is beginning to build momentum. In 1993, the recently formed National Board for Professional Teaching Standards will begin certifying teachers based on their demonstrated professional abilities. Both national teachers unions, the American Federation of Teachers and the National Education Association, have been actively campaigning for greater professional roles for teachers along with increased responsibility and accountability for results. School systems such as those in Miami-Dade County, Rochester, Toledo, and Pittsburgh have been putting these principles into action. In its drive to improve the quality of education statewide, Connecticut has paid particular attention to overhauling its system of teacher preparation, certification, and professional support. Connecticut's reforms are now being used as a model for other states, and together with the University of Pittsburgh, the state was recently awarded the first contract by the National Board for Professional Teaching Standards to develop a model for teacher assessment (see page 63).

Great emphasis has been placed in recent years on providing alternative routes to teacher employment and certification. Although most of the thirty-three states that allow alternative certification routes do so only in cases of teacher shortages, some states are taking a broader approach to recruitment. New Jersey's six-year-old program recruits teacher candidates on college campuses and through local newspaper ads. They teach while completing 200 hours of coursework in one year and are supervised by experienced teachers. By 1989, 29 percent of the state's new teachers had come through this alternative route and as a group scored higher on certification tests than teachers taking traditional routes. In Texas's alter-

---

TEACHER PROFESSIONALIZATION IN CONNECTICUT

The Education Enhancement Act of 1986 helped make teaching in Connecticut a more attractive and rewarding career. The act substantially raised professional standards so that they are now among the highest in the nation, and it increased salaries, making Connecticut teachers the nation's second highest paid.

Provisions of the act included:

The creation of a competency exam for prospective teachers, which is required for admission to teacher-preparation programs and for certification.

Development of an inventory of fifteen competencies that all prospective teachers must demonstrate in order to earn a provisional educator certificate. The competencies include subject matter knowledge and interpersonal skills.

Graduates of teacher-preparation programs are required to major in the specific subject area they plan to teach, rather than in education.

All teacher candidates must pass an examination demonstrating their knowledge of the subject they intend to teach prior to certification.

Special training and financial incentives are provided to experienced teachers who agree to supervise student teachers in their first classroom experience.

The Beginning Education Support and Training (BEST) Program provides support and assessment to beginning teachers. Each new teacher is paired with an experienced colleague who receives specialized training and a stipend to serve as a mentor. At the end of the first year, every new teacher is formally assessed and if passed, receives provisional certification valid for eight years.

The Professional Educator Certificate is earned by teachers who successfully complete thirty hours of study beyond their bachelor of arts degree three years after their provisional certification. To maintain certification, teachers have to complete nine continuing education units every five years.

SOURCE: Connecticut Department of Education.

native program, minority teachers represent 50 percent of those certified in some districts.[10]

Two nongovernmental and highly creative approaches are Teach For America and the Peace Corps fellows program. Teach For America recruits idealistic, top college graduates for a two-year commitment to teach in areas where there is a large shortage of teachers: urban inner cities and rural communities. In the 1990-1991 school year, the first year of the program, over 500 volunteers, who were chosen from 2,500 applicants, have received intensive training from experienced teachers at the University of Southern California and in the Los Angeles school system and were assigned to Los Angeles, New York City, New Orleans, Baton Rouge, and rural Georgia and North Carolina. The Peace Corps is tapping returnees from its international program to teach in inner cities. So far, 60 fellows are enrolled in Columbia University's Teachers College while teaching in New York City, and there are plans to increase the number of participants to 4,000 and expand into several additional states.

We foresee a continuing evolution of the role of the teacher as schools try to restructure to meet the challenges ahead. Out of necessity, schools will have to encourage a broad range of teaching approaches that rely on experienced teachers as learning managers, including the greater use of paraprofessionals and volunteers in the classroom, expansion of team-teaching approaches, and more widespread introduction of advanced learning technologies.

ELEMENTS OF RESTRUCTURED SCHOOLS

Whatever the final outcome of the restructuring process, individual schools will look different, but education systems that are restructured to operate effectively and productively in a new society should have a number of characteristics in common. They include the following:

A safe and stimulating school environment. Schools should promote creativity and learning; be orderly, physically inviting, free of drugs and violence; and have a positive invisible curriculum. The school environment should also reduce anonymity for students and increase their level of interaction with caring adults.

Performance-based goals to measure the effectiveness of the system against agreed-upon performance standards.

Incentives for performance for teachers, administrators, and students.

A process for school-based decision making that allows for maximum flexibility and accountability and that involves principals, teachers, parents, students, and other school personnel.

Teachers with high standards and a high level of professional competence and responsibility who are committed to learning and the development of children and adolescents. Teachers in schools that serve the disadvantaged should also have experience and expertise in dealing with children with multiple problems.

Increased parental involvement in both school decision making and the progress of their own children.

A curriculum that balances the teaching of the basics of what should be mastered in a communications-based, more highly technological society with variations that reflect local needs and individual interests and pursuits.

An emphasis on English language proficiency as a goal for all students. Foreign language skills are important, especially in an increasingly global marketplace. Bilingual education is necessary for students who enter schools without sufficient English language skills, but all children need to become proficient in English.

Active support of preschool and child care programs whether community-based or run by the schools themselves to help prepare children to be effective and eager learners.

Social support systems linked to schools that provide necessary human services, including health care, nutritional supplements, and psychological, career, and family counseling.

Better and more widespread use of up-to-date education technology integrated into the curriculum to provide new learning opportunities and more individualized attention for students and additional pedagogical support for teachers.

Increased emphasis on extracurricular activities that help build academic, social, and physical skills.

Increased choices among public schools to allow students to attend the school that best matches their learning needs and interests.

Chapter 4

CREATING CHANGE

Business has a critical role to play in creating the positive political climate needed for improving the quality of government policies and practices, of which education and child development form an important part. No change in public policy can occur without a sizable political constituency. Unless key community leaders can forge a broad-enough coalition or a critical mass of support from the voting public, it is doubtful that a particular public policy agenda, no matter how worthy, will be politically feasible.

THE IMPACT OF EDUCATION REFORM

In the past decade, reform initiatives have been introduced at every level of education policy and practice, including state and federal government, local school districts, and individual schools. Every sector has been involved – education, government, business, private foundations, and community organizations. Although the results of much of this activity have been inconclusive, some important gains have been made.

STATE LEADERSHIP

Nearly every state is at some stage of seriously addressing its educational problems. For example:

- Nearly every state now has some form of statewide student-accountability testing. Some states, such as Georgia and Florida, expanded existing programs; and others, such as Pennsylvania and Ohio, mandated statewide student testing for the first time.

- Forty-three states have increased or specified for the first time their high school graduation requirements.

- Thirty-three states have some alternative route to teacher certification that allows qualified individuals to bypass traditional state-certified teacher-training programs. As recently as 1983, only eight states provided such alternative routes.

- More than twenty states have passed or are considering legislation to expand public school choice.

- About twenty states are in the process of redesigning their school-funding systems in order to distribute funds more equitably to less wealthy districts.

- Nine states (New Jersey, Ohio, Arkansas, Georgia, Kentucky, New Mexico, South Carolina, Texas, and West Virginia) have enacted provisions for intervening in academically bankrupt districts.

- More than two-thirds of the states have taken steps to reduce the incidence and costs of teen pregnancy, and nineteen states have expanded Medicare coverage to include pregnant women and young children in families with incomes up to 133 percent of the federal poverty level.

In addition, the President and the National Governors' Association have provided leadership on both education and early childhood development by formulating and promoting a sweeping set of national goals for education. Significantly, these goals recognized both the importance of better preparing children for education and the need to restructure schools to make them more accountable for their performance.

LOCAL ACTION

Some of the most innovative developments are taking place at the local level, particularly in the large urban school districts and in individual schools. Urban districts such as Miami, Rochester, and Toledo have taken the lead in upgrading the teaching profession.

School-based management has become a popular strategy for responding with greater flexibility to the educational needs of children. This strategy usually goes hand in hand with measures to increase teacher professionalism and accountability. School-based management, which was pioneered in Miami-Dade County, is being utilized by growing numbers of large urban districts, including New York City, Los Angeles, and Boston.

Other school systems, such as New Haven, Hartford, and Prince Georges County, have experimented successfully with improving parental participation in schools using the process developed by Dr. James P. Comer. The Rockefeller Foundation is providing $15 million to help Dr. Comer bring his school-reform process to a broader constituency of local schools. Still other individual schools are experimenting with a variety of innovative ideas. One of the most promising is the ungraded elementary school championed by the Coalition for Essential Schools and supported by the Education Commission of the States through its Re: Learning project. Schools in six states (Arkansas, Delaware, Illinois, New Mexico, Pennsylvania, and Rhode Island) are taking part in Re: Learning.

A CRITICAL ROLE FOR BUSINESS

The business community has become a major champion of education reform and has led the calls for both restructuring education and investing in prevention and intervention for the disadvantaged. Much of the impetus for business involvement has stemmed from CED's first two policy reports on education reform, *Investing in Our Children* and *Children in Need*.[1] *Investing in Our Children* asserted that education should not be considered an expense but recognized as an investment with a substantial payoff for the nation's future and offered a blueprint for bottom-up reform of the public schools. *Children in Need* addressed the special needs of disadvantaged children, who were being largely bypassed by education reform. CED called on business to take a strong role as an advocate of early and sustained intervention strategies to break the cycle of failure.

Business leadership has provided the impetus for many state and local reform initiatives, and in a majority of these cases, business involvement is credited with making the difference between success and failure.[2] South Carolina, Minnesota, Boston, Chicago, and Miami provide good examples of long-term reform that would not have occurred without the support and involvement of the business community.

There are many thousands of new business-sponsored projects in more than a third of the nation's schools, with notable concentrations in areas of urban poverty. In all, there are over 140,000 partnerships in over 30,000 schools, and more than half involve business.

Although small and medium-sized firms are involved in the vast majority of school partnerships, a number of the nation's largest corporations are making financial commitments of unprecedented size to school-improvement efforts. Recently, multimillion-dollar programs have been announced by five Fortune 100 corporations. General Electric has set aside $20 million to double the number of disadvantaged youths in its College Bound program; RJR Nabisco is offering $30 million over a five-year period through its Next Century Schools project to help spur innovation on a school-by-school basis; Coca-Cola has committed at least $5 million a year for the next decade to support a variety of programs, including minority education, innovations in urban education, leadership training for secondary school teachers, and literacy programs; and Citibank is committing $20 million over the next ten years to a variety of strategies and programs for school improvement (see page 69).

In a number of communities, such as Boston and Chicago, business leaders have taken the initiative in developing and promoting reforms. Chicago's radical school-restructuring plan, which decentralizes the school system down to the school-building level, resulted in part from the growing politicization of the city's business community. Chicago's reform effort is very new and it will be some time before any improvements may be seen in student achievement. However, two lessons can now be derived from the experience: First, communities can decide that they will no longer tolerate dysfunctional schools and can muster the political will necessary to radically restructure the schools. Second, where the political will is strong enough, schools can be changed in any way, no matter how different, that the community decides is needed (see page 70).[3]

The Boston Compact provides another example of how a committed business community can take the initiative to demand structural change

---

CITIBANK: BANKING ON EDUCATION

Since 1983, Citibank has been funding a wide array of experimental projects for kindergarten through grade twelve. Although there have been favorable results on a project-by-project basis, the bank has been frustrated by an inability to see real sustained improvement.

In order to make an impact on the education system, Citibank has committed $20 million dollars for the next ten years to its Banking on Education program and will redirect $2 million a year in existing funds. The goal of the program is to improve student performance and stimulate systemwide reform.

The first $10 million will be spent on ensuring that every child in its ten partnership schools in Citibank communities throughout New York, Chicago, Houston, and Los Angeles is either college-ready or work-ready. To accomplish this objective, students will be given tutoring and preparation for the Scholastic Aptitude Test to prepare them for college or co-op and work-study programs for the work-ready track. Each student will be assigned a Citibank mentor for guidance.

The second $10 million will be committed to stimulating system-wide reform. Of this, $7.2 million will go to thirty designated school-based management schools in Chicago, Washington, D.C., and the Miami area, and $3.0 million will go to Ted Sizer at Brown University to expand his Coalition of Essential Schools. The money will be used to fund 100 Citibank Fellows, veteran teachers who will teach new Coalition teachers principles such as getting students to take more responsibility for their education and learning how to think.

SOURCE: Citibank Foundation.

in school organization. In the eight years since it was first established, the Boston Compact has undergone a major transformation. What began as an incentive program linking gains in student achievement to job opportunities has evolved into a program for restructuring the city's schools by introducing school-based management and a form of public school choice. At each stage of the Compact's evolution, changes have been demanded by the business community in exchange for its continued support.

EDUCATION REFORM IN CHICAGO

The Chicago school system underwent a radical change at the start of the 1989-90 school year. After months of lobbying by a coalition of business leaders, education advocates, and parents in all income brackets, the Illinois legislature settled on legislation that transfers power from a top-heavy bureaucracy to lay control. The change grew out of deep frustration with the system: 70 percent of Chicago public school students are from families below the poverty level, the dropout rate is 45 percent, and the average test score of students in nearly half the schools was in the bottom 1 percent in the nation in 1987.

Each school is now run by a parent-led council with the far-reaching authority previously held by the Board of Education. These Local School Councils (LCSs) consist of six parents, two community residents with no children in the school, and two teachers, all elected to two-year terms. Principals sit on the councils but have no say on their appointment or dismissal, a decision that requires seven votes. The LSCs also have the power to approve budgets and make recommendations on books and curricula.

This decentralized school system weakens the role of newly elected Superintendent Ted D. Kimbrough and the Board of Education and gives Mayor Richard M. Daley the leading voice on school policy. However, the law did leave the Board of Education a key lever over the councils. The board can close a school if a council fails in its duties.

The Chicago experiment recently suffered a setback when the Illinois Supreme Court ruled the reform act unconstitutional because the method used to elect the members of the local school councils violated the principle of one person, one vote. To rectify the situation, the legislature passed a revised version of the reform act in January 1991 and gave itself six months to correct problems in the election procedures.

SOURCES: *Chicago Enterprise*, February 1990 and February 1991, and *New York Times*, September 3, 1989.

ACTION ON EARLY CHILDHOOD DEVELOPMENT

The wisdom of providing preschool preparation and other forms of early intervention for disadvantaged children has emerged as a key theme for education reform. In 1990, Head Start, the flagship early intervention program for three- to five-year-olds, received the largest funding increase in its history, and Congress voted full-funding authorization for the program by 1994. At least thirty-five states now fund some sort of preschool program, up from only eight a decade ago, and some forty-five states have implemented legislation that specifically addresses the problems of at-risk children. But numbers have not yet been matched by results, and most legislation targeted to disadvantaged children is piecemeal in nature, typically supporting only a limited number of pilot programs.[4]

A handful of states and local communities are attempting to address early childhood development in a more coherent and coordinated fashion. The Minneapolis Success by 6 project (see page 72), Florida's Save the Children legislative package, New Jersey's Invest in Children project, and Connecticut's 1-2-3-4-5 Kids Count initiative (see page 73) are excellent examples of ways in which communities are linking their future economic competitiveness to the well-being of their children.

BUSINESS AND THE DISADVANTAGED

In *Children in Need*, CED urged business to become the primary advocate of disadvantaged children in the community because these children lack the political voice to speak out for themselves. Business support for preschool and other early childhood intervention programs has been shown to be critical for creating the political will required to implement and fund these programs at the national, state, and local levels. Increasingly, businesses are shaping their policies toward education and devoting additional corporate resources with the needs of disadvantaged children in mind. For example, Primerica, Inc., joined forces with the Children's Defense Fund on a major national campaign on behalf of full funding for Head Start. GE focuses the major share of its educational efforts on identifying and supporting minority students with math and science aptitude. In Hartford, Connecticut, The Travelers Companies have organized a consortium of public- and private-sector organizations into the Hartford Early Learning Partnership. In Tulsa, Oklahoma, the business community is spearheading a drive to establish a citywide child care system within the public schools. In Dallas, the Texas Instruments Foundation has joined with Head Start to sponsor a model quality preschool program (see page 74).

MINNEAPOLIS SUCCESS BY 6: THE FIRST 15 MONTHS

Success by 6, created by United Way of Minneapolis, recognizes that the best investment in a child's later success in school is the earliest investment that can be made. The Success by 6 initiative has created a powerful coalition of advocates for children under age six in Minneapolis in which business leaders play a central role.

The program's goals are to improve public information, policies, and programs that address the social, educational, health care, and emotional needs of children from the earliest stages of prenatal care to age six, when they enter school. In its first fifteen months of operation, Success by 6 successfully initiated all of its original goals and strategies, which included:

Improving community support by creating an understanding of the crisis, building a broad bipartisan legislative agenda, and expanding the ability of employers to help parents balance work and family.

Improving access to services by expanding and coordinating services for families with young children, training parents and caregivers in early development, and providing access to prenatal care for more women.

Improving collaboration by strengthening community leadership, replicating Success by 6 throughout the community, and expanding support and recognition for culturally sensitive programs.

The Minneapolis Chamber of Commerce, Minnesota Business Partnership, Junior League, Honeywell, Northwest Hennepin Human Services Council, and the Minneapolis Youth Coordinating Board are all playing major roles in Success by 6 action strategies. Among the initial accomplishments of Success by 6 is the creation of Way to Grow, a program model for coordination of services, that is already serving fifty families in a pilot program in the low-income Minneapolis neighborhood of Phillips.

In addition, a strong legislative agenda that was developed with the support of thirty-five advocates for youths and young children resulted in a $35.6 million increase in support for young children.

Success by 6 Northwest is expanding the Success by 6 model to the Minneapolis suburbs to identify and address suburban barriers and issues in early childhood development.

SOURCE: Minneapolis United Way.

Although the issue of early intervention to help the disadvantaged has emerged as a major theme of education reform, few real changes have been made in policies or programs for disadvantaged children that would achieve positive results on any broad scale. In spite of increased activity on the part of individual business leaders and companies, the business community has not yet rallied to the cause of early intervention to the extent that it has supported school reform. The CED research project on the impact of business involvement in education reform identified three reasons for this tepid response: First, business has had a later start on this issue. Second, there is no one institution comparable to the schools that

---

1,2,3,4,5, KIDS COUNT

In Connecticut, state and local government, community leaders, families, and the private sector are working together to combat the problems of the most vulnerable segment of its population: children from birth to age five. Kids Count is authorized by state legislation and is supported by foundation grants.

The first phase of the project's statewide campaign researched existing state services for young children and their families in the areas of child care and early childhood education, maternal and infant health, mental health, family support programs, parks and recreation, and library services.

The data gathered are being used to shape a model policy package of early childhood and family support legislation at the state level and a policy package for mayors. Technical assistance is being provided to help municipalities view their towns from the perspective of children and families. Cost-effective strategies are being developed to improve program coordination and content, and the project is working to build bridges between state and local initiatives and secure the active cooperation of parents and city leaders.

In its second phase, there will be a statewide bilingual media campaign on the importance of the early years for children who are healthy, motivated, and ready for school. A multiracial team of outreach workers will be set up to work in targeted areas to encourage parental involvement and to strengthen families. The Business Advisory Committee will provide a strong advocacy voice for early childhood issues and will design a cost-benefit analysis of early childhood programs for the state.

SOURCE: Connecticut Commission on Children.

encompasses early childhood development with which business can interact directly. Third, the up-front cost and complexity of dealing with the problems of young children and their families seem overwhelming.[5]

We believe that much more must be done, and it must be done quickly. Those children who are born today will enter kindergarten in 1996 and will not graduate from high school until 2009 – if, indeed, they make it that far. For the 25 percent born into poverty and the one in four growing up in a single-parent home, the odds are stacked against them. These children need more than education reform. They need an early and sustained intervention in their lives to help them break the vicious cycle of poverty and stay on track.

We call on business to focus its energies on improving education

---

DALLAS MODEL PRESCHOOL

In Dallas, the Texas Instruments Foundation joined with Head Start to sponsor the Margaret H. Cone Center, a model quality preschool program, which opened in March 1990 with eighty-six children. Also involved were the Meadows Foundation, the Communities Foundation, the University of Texas at Arlington, and the Julius C. Freezer Elementary School. The full-day (nine-hour) year-round program costs about $5,737 per child and is open to all four-year-olds in the elementary school zone. Head Start provides $3,000 per child, and Texas Instruments provides $2,737 per child, or $288,000 annually to support the preschool program.

The model program supplements the usual Head Start program in several important ways. A nurse-practitioner on staff actively seeks to provide all the health and dental services that the children may require. There are two social workers on staff at the preschool who provide social services for the children and their families using case-management strategies. Employment counseling is also provided. Four parents are currently enrolled in a GED program and eleven others recently completed the Paid Parent Program, a four-hour-a-day program to become a Head Start teacher's aide.

An early childhood development specialist, who has a bachelor's degree, serves as the assistant director of the center and works with teachers who have only associate-level certification. Teachers make home visits to the parents to keep them in touch with the progress of their children, and parents are required to devote one hour per semester to volunteer work at the center.

SOURCE: Texas Instruments Foundation.

and child development for all children while giving highest priority to meeting the needs of the disadvantaged.

Business should support policy change at the federal, state, and municipal levels. It should also initiate activities that will have a direct impact on the education and development of the children of its employees and the children in the communities in which it operates.

In looking to the long-term development of a pool of quality potential employees, business should promote rational public-sector efforts that coordinate a comprehensive set of policies covering child care, child development, parental education and support, and health care to address the needs of today's families with children.

Business should also review its internal policies in such areas as family benefits and support for parent involvement in children's development and education to ensure that they are consistent with its external policies on education and children's issues.

Furthermore, the general crisis in the overall quality of education is evident, and we urge the business community to continue to focus its efforts on the broad education-improvement agenda in order to ensure that every child will become a successful, productive, and responsible adult.

RESULTS OF REFORM

While education-reform activity has increased dramatically, the payoff in terms of improved educational achievement has hardly been realized. We see several reasons for this.

First, very few reform initiatives have been in place long enough to have had a sustained impact on student achievement. The decline in educational achievement occurred over several decades, and it would be unrealistic to expect the solution to take hold after only a few short years.

Second, few state reform strategies are coordinated or coherent. A recent study found that most state reform efforts contain unrelated provisions, sending conflicting messages to schools without setting clear priorities; most place a layer of new reforms on top of old without taking the time or effort to evaluate whether earlier reforms are producing results; and most avoid more complex reforms that require additional funding in favor of those that are more manageable and call for little or no new funds. [6]

Third, and most important, few state or local initiatives address the complex developmental needs of children as part of their overall strategy to improve education. Most restructuring efforts focus exclusively on the schools and continue to treat education and learning as if they do not begin until age four or five.

In those few states and localities where there has been long-term commitment to structural change, the payoffs are beginning to be noticeable. In states such as California and South Carolina, where reform has been under way for at least five years, student achievement is beginning to show substantial gains. Although the path of reform in California has not proceeded smoothly, steady gains are beginning to be seen nevertheless. Since 1986, the scores of eighth graders in reading and mathematics have risen 25 percent, the dropout rate has decreased by 18 percent, and the number of graduates qualifying for entrance into the University of California has risen 20 percent.[7]

In South Carolina, students and schools have made significant gains since 1983 in the eight areas targeted for improvement and in meeting the six general goals of the EIA. The number of students meeting the exit examination requirements has increased 40 percent; writing performance is up by 11 percent; student absences are down by 20 percent; more than three times as many students are taking advanced courses; substantial gains have been posted in SAT scores; and the rate at which students are attending college has increased by 7 percent. Equally important, opinion polls indicate that parent, teacher, and business-community confidence in the South Carolina schools has increased dramatically. Almost 70 percent of business leaders surveyed in the summer of 1989 felt that the EIA had a positive impact on their businesses. Nevertheless, improving education is still considered a pressing issue, and the governor, legislature, and business community continue to work together to reassess and redirect reform strategies.

What is most significant about the reform process in both California and South Carolina is that it has been intensive, systematic, goal-oriented, and self-renewing and has enjoyed the widespread support and involvement of the state's business and civic communities. In addition, both states have recognized the importance of early childhood development and have continued to increase their emphasis on earlier intervention with preschool children and their families.

More states, such as Kentucky, Ohio, and Oklahoma, are now attempting to develop a more coordinated approach to education reform. Kentucky has chosen to avoid a threatened court takeover because of glaring inequities in its school financing system and used this situation as an opportunity to overhaul the entire state education system to emphasize educational goals, assessment of results, and performance-based rewards and sanctions (see page 77).

EDUCATION REFORM IN KENTUCKY

On March 29, 1990, Kentucky enacted the most sweeping education package ever conceived by a state legislature. All current educational regulations have been declared unconstitutional by the Kentucky Supreme Court because of wide disparities in spending between rich and poor districts and are repealed under the reform bill. By 1996, the state's 178 school districts must surrender control of local school budgets and educational programs to local boards consisting of three teachers, two parents, and an administrator. To comply with the court order, the state will develop a procedure to make local tax rates uniform. In addition, the reform bill includes the following elements:

Goals. The state's new role will be to set forth seven capacities for all students to acquire, including communication skills, knowledge, citizenship, self-assurance, tolerance, wisdom, and competitiveness. The state board of education will circulate a model curriculum that will be a guide for schools to follow, not a mandate. Individual school districts and schools will be free to determine how to meet the seven proposed goals and will have decision-making power on courses, textbooks, and supporting materials.

Assessments. By the 1995-96 school year, the state board of education shall implement a performance-based assessment program that requires local school boards to publish annual performance reports. Rather than determining student achievement through standardized multiple-choice tests, students will be asked to demonstrate their writing skills or their understanding of a concept in science or math. This kind of assessment program will require a better kind of teaching than one that focuses on choosing the correct answer from a list.

Rewards/Sanctions. The state education department will adopt a formula to determine successful schools based on the percentage of successful students. Certified staff shall decide how to allot the financial awards.

In a school defined as "in crisis," certified staff will be placed on probation, students will have the option of transferring to a successful school, and distinguished educators will be assigned to assist staff with implementing a school-improvement plan. The school may appeal the performance judgment, and the board may adjust it.

SOURCES: Summary of The Kentucky Education Reform Act of 1990 and *New York Times*, April 4, May 6, and June 8, 1990.

THE FEDERAL ROLE

Although education in the United States is primarily a state and local responsibility, the federal government has an important role to play both in setting education policy and in providing funds for a variety of education and child development programs that focus on the needs of the disadvantaged.

Currently, the federal government provides only between 6 and 7 percent of all school funding. Nevertheless, the actions taken by the federal government play a critical leadership role in setting the tone and pace for reform. A key example of such leadership has been the development of national education goals by President Bush and the nation's governors, an effort that has served to create a deep sense of urgency throughout the nation on the need to develop strategies for meeting the six goals (see Chapter 3, pages 43-44).

Of paramount importance is the role the federal government must continue to play in ensuring the disadvantaged access to quality education. Without equity, there can be no real excellence in education. We believe that full funding of Head Start should continue to be a federal priority. The federal government should also ensure adequate funding for those programs that have proven to be good educational investments, such as the Women, Infants, and Children's (WIC) nutrition program and immunizations against childhood diseases that can cause permanent health damage. In addition:

- Federal leadership is critical for conveying the message to state and local government, to educators and parents, and to the voting public that child development and education policies and programs deserve top priority.

- Data collection and research at the federal level are crucial for continued innovation in education and children's programs, particularly in such areas as measurement and testing, pedagogy, technology use and access, and programs targeted to the disadvantaged. We urge Congress to support the expansion of the NAEP to enable it to explore new assessment tools and to provide state-by-state comparisons of achievement data.

- Actions by the federal government can improve the flexibility of program administration and funding at every level of government and can increase access to these programs for children and parents who need them. The federal government can both provide the impetus to state governments to streamline their service-delivery systems and make it easier for state and local governments to utilize federal funds more flexibly and effectively.

THE ROLE OF THE PRIVATE VOLUNTARY SECTOR

The private voluntary sector plays a vital role in developing and sustaining programs for children and families and in education. Representing an extremely broad range of organizations – from grass-roots neighborhood associations to comprehensive family service centers and from foundations to religious organizations – private voluntary organizations often serve as the critical intermediary between business, education, and government in developing and initiating programs and linking the resources of a variety of public and private institutions.

These organizations provide a wide range of services essential to attaining the nation's education goals, including quality preschool, parenting programs, mentoring, tutoring, youth development, gang intervention, drug-abuse prevention and treatment, and many more.

Voluntary health and human service organizations often play a pivotal role in ensuring the development of disadvantaged children through the many and varied programs they run for these children and their families. For example, the YMCA in Manchester, New Hampshire, runs an alternative school for children who have failed the seventh grade and are at risk of becoming dropouts. This school provides intense instruction in seventh- and eighth-grade material combined with counseling and enrichment activities that prepare the children to rejoin their classmates in the ninth grade. None of these children have subsequently dropped out of school, and some have become honor students.

The Healthy Mothers/Healthy Babies program in Lancaster, South Carolina, is a collaboration between the county health department, voluntary human service agencies, and the United Way to provide health care, education, parenting skills training, and counseling to teen mothers. It operates through a clinic next to the high school with the highest pregnancy rate in the county. A major program goal is to help young mothers return to school and avoid a second pregnancy.

In Tampa, Florida, the Boys and Girls Clubs run a homework-assistance program in ten neighborhoods. The program helps children with their homework assignments, builds self-esteem, and encourages aspirations toward higher education.

In 1990, the worldwide service organization Kiwanis International initiated Young Children: Priority One, a three-year program that will focus the resources of 8,400 Kiwanis Clubs in the United States and abroad on meeting the needs of children from before birth through age five. Kiwanis International is providing information and technical assistance to the local clubs to help them design projects and develop collaborations with other organizations, resources, and leaders in their communities.

In a project called Say Yes to a Youngster's Future, the National Urban Coalition is working with minority and female students to increase

---

UNITED WAY OF AMERICA

Present in over 2,400 communities across the country, United Way is an excellent resource for developing partnerships with business and government in education, child development, and the human services. In 1989, United Ways raised nearly $3 billion to support over 40,000 local voluntary health and human service agencies. In many communities, United Way serves as a focal point for mobilizing and coordinating community action on the developmental needs of children of all ages, especially the disadvantaged.

Just as United Way of Minneapolis worked in partnership with Honeywell to rally the community around early childhood needs, other United Ways have taken the lead in convening coalitions in their communities. These collaborations are addressing education-related problems such as dropout rates, drug abuse, gang involvement, and teen pregnancy, in addition to early childhood development.

United Way is a good community resource for coalition building because it has:

- Broad-based access to all sectors of the community.

- Links with the broad spectrum of service providers and advocates that work with at-risk children and their families.

- Active involvement of great numbers of volunteer leaders from all parts of the community who are already committed and working to make the community a better place to live and work.

- A neutral table around which all segments of the community – government, educators, minority groups, human service agencies, business, and labor – can work together to address pressing problems.

SOURCE: United Way of America.

their exposure to and interest in mathematics, science, and technology. The project is run in partnership with school districts in Washington, D.C., Houston, and New Orleans, and parents and teachers participate in special programs with the children that emphasize hands-on learning activities. The Shell Oil Corporation has helped to get this program under way.

In Connecticut, United Way and voluntary service agencies are helping the state to promote and support the establishment of Family Resource Centers in the schools. These centers provide year-round child care, parenting workshops, literacy training, and much more. United Way helps to support these centers financially and also links voluntary services with the centers.

A new national partnership between business and the voluntary sector is One to One, a collaboration between United Way of America and the One to One Foundation. This program was formed to bring together existing resources, organizations, and leaders in an innovative fashion to create new partnerships to help disadvantaged youths through mentoring and entrepreneurial activities. At the local level, One to One is establishing Leadership Councils with business, government, and voluntary support to promote and coordinate mentoring and ensure that every at-risk young person has access to a caring adult mentor. Many of these councils are being established through the leadership of Goldman, Sachs & Co.

Business and the private voluntary sector can work together most effectively to reinforce each other's efforts in addressing the problems of education and the needs of children. Business, in looking to expand its involvement in hands-on programs, can benefit greatly from the resources and expertise of the private voluntary organizations. At the same time, business can provide these organizations with leadership, financial support, and help in recruiting volunteers from among its employees.

THE ROLE OF BUSINESS AT THE STATE LEVEL

Perhaps the most important target for direct business involvement in public policy is structural change in education and child development systems at the state level. CED's research on the impact of business involvement in education and child development reform clearly shows that business support of state and local education efforts has often spelled the difference between success and failure.

Legislative control and responsibility for almost everything that happens in the public schools rests at the state level. Major parts of the responsibility for both the funding and the management of schools may have been delegated to individual districts, but in most cases the state has the authority to determine academic standards, curriculum, graduation requirements, and base salaries and certification requirements for teachers, and to establish choice programs. If the political will exists, the state has the authority to see that almost every recommendation for school improvement is implemented throughout the state.

For most states, public education is by far the largest item in the budget and therefore involves many vested interests who are quite influential and may be resistant to change. They range from the obvious, such as the teacher and administrator unions and textbook publishers, to the obscure, such as food service and transportation providers.

Structural change in education is unlikely to occur without strong and committed political leadership from the business community. Business can bring its own influence to bear and, even more important, can bring the reform movement credibility with the voting public, who must be moved to support change if public officials are to take it seriously.

The Business Roundtable (BRT), an organization that represents the chief executive officers (CEOs) of 213 major corporations, is taking a major role in bringing business leadership to state-level education reform. Under the leadership of IBM Chairman John Akers, the BRT has recently made an unprecedented ten-year commitment to restructuring education at the state level. For each state, one or more Roundtable CEOs have volunteered to work with the governor, other top state political leaders, and other interested parties to identify the key education problems, develop a strategy for addressing them, and work to implement the necessary policy, regulatory, and funding changes. To support the CEOs in this effort, the BRT has designed a series of CEO-governor dialogues hosted by the Aspen Institute. In addition, both CED and the National Alliance of Business have joined with the BRT in producing publications on the role of business in state education reform and in restructuring education.[8]

CONSTITUENCY BUILDING [9]

The most important first step toward change is to create a constituency for reform and maintain its interest over the long term. The process for building a constituency for change is the same, whether it seeks to address child development policies or education reform or whether it takes place at the state or the local level. There are ten essential steps.

1. Cultivate the commitment of top political and business leaders to the importance of structural reform. The most important political leaders include the governor, the speaker of the state house of representatives, and the president of the state senate. Key business leaders include the heads of the state's leading employers and those involved with the state's Business Roundtable, Chamber of Commerce, or other business groups. When the new New York City Schools Chancellor Joseph Fernandez needed changes in state law to carry out his reform agenda, the New York business community rallied to his support and successfully lobbied the legislature for the required changes.

2. Broaden the base of support by developing a coalition or partnership. This coalition should include key leaders of interested constituencies, such as business, teachers, school administrators, parents, board of education members, minorities, central cities, suburbs, rural communities, child and family advocates, key intermediary groups, key legislators from both political parties, and the superintendent of schools.

In one of the most populous counties in New York State, the Westchester Education Coalition, an alliance of Westchester-based corporations, local school systems, education organizations, social services, and child and family advocates, focused on enhancing the quality of education by serving as a resource and a catalyst for change. The coalition conducts a broad-ranging program of activities that include providing mentors for at-risk students, offering minigrants to teachers and principals for creative solutions to classroom problems, and providing support directly to school districts in the process of restructuring. One corporate coalition member, NYNEX, is currently making top-quality management training in shared decision making, team building, and communications available without cost to teachers and administrators in the Port Chester school district.

Two new collaborative projects in New Orleans are working toward structural reform of the school system and improving the development of children and their readiness for school. With funding from the corporate community, the Coalition for Educational Excellence by 2000 (Co-Ed 2000) has brought together a planning team consisting of the school board president, the superintendent of schools, the president of the teachers' union and business and civic leaders to address the underlying problems of the school system and bring about long-term structural improvement. One of the primary goals of Co-Ed 2000 is to provide school leaders with the training and support they will need in order to bring about institutional change. A related business, education, and community collaboration, the New Orleans Council for Young Children in Need, is attempting to create a more coordinated system of services to address the developmental needs of children in their first five years (see page 84).

3. Diagnose the problem, but do not fix blame on any one constituency or group.

- Determine what the desirable educational outcomes ought to be for adequate preparation for citizenship, productive work, and other adult responsibilities, such as family life.

- Analyze the changing demographics of the child and adult population, the work force, and the educational system.

- Assess the state's existing range of programs and policies that bear

---

THE NEW ORLEANS COUNCIL FOR YOUNG CHILDREN IN NEED

The New Orleans Council For Young Children In Need was founded in 1987 by a local businessman in recognition of the relationship between the well-being of the city's children and the vitality of the community. The mission of the organization is to maximize the potential of children in need from the prenatal stage through age five by establishing a child development service system that addresses a variety of needs of children and their families in Orleans Parish.

The Council convened two seminars on early intervention and published a widely circulated report entitled "Early Intervention Strategies for the 90's." The strategy plan became the foundation of the Council, and three key partners, The Junior League, the Public Schools, and the City, have agreed to fund the council with a start-up budget of $100,000 per year. A grant from the Greater New Orleans Foundation and this initial funding package enabled the Council to hire an executive director and establish a permanent office.

Specific goals being undertaken by the Council include: the publication of user-friendly guides to services for young children by neighborhood; a public awareness campaign focusing on the benefits of early intervention; and a resource tracking center to help service providers locate and apply for available public and private dollars. The Council will also monitor and facilitate the implementation of publicly funded programs that have an impact on young children and will advocate for increased funding for services for young children in need and their families. The Council is also planning to develop a model for the coordination and delivery of comprehensive services that can be replicated throughout the community.

SOURCE: New Orleans Council for Young Children In Need.

on education, human resource development, and work force preparation.

- Assess prior experience with reform efforts at the state and local levels and how well or poorly these are working. Examine successful reform initiatives in other states to determine effective strategies and utilize whatever work has already been done to analyze the problem and develop solutions.

The first step taken by Minneapolis United Way in developing its Success by 6 project was to conduct an assessment of community needs. This is a slow process that sometimes seems to delay action. Nevertheless, needs assessment allowed Success by 6 to develop a better strategy based on a clear understanding of which programs already existed, what gaps remained, and what barriers impeded the implementation of necessary new policies and programs.

4. Develop a clear vision of what a new system of education and child development should look like. Achieving significant reform will require sustained hard work on complex and detailed issues over a long period of time. In developing a broad vision, it is helpful to examine the following strategic issues: goals and results, governance and management, resources, content, the needs of special groups such as the educationally disadvantaged, the integration of related programs, and performance assessment. Kentucky and Ohio provide two good examples of states that have redesigned their education systems by first developing a clear understanding of what the state's educational goals should be.

5. Determine a reform strategy. The strategies for achieving the vision should be as carefully thought out as the vision itself and should receive at least as much consideration as any serious, long-term business plan. The strategy should clearly identify its own goals and objectives based on an assessment of the key leverage points on which the education-reform coalition should press. It should identify priorities that will concentrate effort as well as resources, tasks, assignments, timetables, benchmarks, and ways of measuring its own performance over time.

Some business leaders will have special expertise to offer. For example, personal experience with corporate restructuring may provide insight into the feasibility of various strategies to restructure the school system. Or as an employer of entry-level workers, a business leader may have a special interest in identifying what students should know and be able to do to be productive workers. IBM, for example, is focusing its national education strategy on increasing access to information technology for schools in disadvantaged areas.

6. Promote the reform agenda. With its visibility, credibility, resources, and political clout, business can play a major role in promoting the reform agenda and building support for its adoption and implementation. It can act as a catalyst and intermediary to bring together groups across a broad spectrum to enlarge and strengthen the reform coalition.

Aggressive public education campaigns may be required to persuade the public and voters of the importance of reform proposals. One of business's strongest assets is its marketing expertise. It should use this expertise to promote reform in education and child development policies in the community. In South Carolina, for example, the business community spent considerable resources promoting the education-reform package through a comprehensive information and advertising campaign and by conducting extensive town meetings throughout the state to build public support.

The media are an important asset in getting the message across to the public. Business leaders may have, or could develop, access to and good working relationships with reporters and editors assigned to, or with an interest in, education topics. Business may also communicate directly with supporters, opinion leaders, and the public through direct mail and mass advertisements. In addition to substantially increasing its reporting of national education news in the past few years, the *New York Times* has run an exemplary series in its metropolitan section called "Against the Odds," focusing on the successes of one particular inner-city school in the Bronx. Also in the New York and New Jersey areas, one of the local independent television stations, WWOR-TV, has committed substantial airtime and financial resources to supporting education through its "A+ for Kids" program.

7. Press for Implementation. Some reform initiatives focus on specific legislative goals, such as passing a law or getting a tax increase, and assume that once that goal is achieved, the job is done. Unfortunately, this is not necessarily so. Once a law is passed, it is easy to mistakenly assume that it will be implemented or, if implemented, that it will achieve its intended result. Implementation can be stalled at any one of several junctures:

- At the state level, by the board of education, state superintendent of schools, and various agencies of the state department of education or other state agencies.

- At the local level, by the local board of education, superintendent of schools, and various assistant superintendents and associated agencies of the central school administration.

- In a large local school system, by decentralized area offices or even neighborhood school districts, some of which have separately elected boards.

- At the school level, by the principal and other administrators, Parent-Teacher Associations, and other advisory boards, as well as teachers, school service workers, and unions.

- In local general-purpose governments, which have important administrative power, if the school system is an agency of the local government or depends on it for its budget approval and funding.

Absence of follow-up is one of the weak links in reform efforts. Follow-up activities are sometimes tedious and time-consuming and require political and administrative expertise and savvy. They are rarely recognized for the important contributions they make. This is precisely why business, with its seriousness of purpose and long-term commitment to practical action, can play such a critical role in this aspect of reform. In Ohio and South Carolina, the restructuring agenda included establishing assessment committees of business and civic leaders to monitor the results of the reform effort and, when necessary, recommend new strategies for change.

8. Participate directly in substantive efforts. Many of the more highly publicized business-education reform efforts have been those that involve direct participation in the schools or in other substantive areas of education. These range from minor to major projects: adopt-a-school programs, exposure of students to the workplace, mentoring, experimentation with new learning methods and technologies, and the establishment of independent schools and programs. An excellent example of this kind of hands-on activity is the national network of Academies of Finance, founded by American Express in 1982 and supported by a consortium of over 200 companies through the National Academy Foundation (see page 88). Business also has expertise in management and resource allocation that would be useful for improving the governance of education at the school district and local school levels. In years past, business people in high managerial positions regularly served on school boards; but for a variety of reasons, few currently do. Companies should provide incentives for top managers to run for school board seats in order to provide this kind of direct management expertise.

Managerial expertise is also very useful to principals and teachers involved in school-based management at the school-building level. For many years, IBM has run a principals' academy for the Washington, D.C., school system. In New York City, IBM is providing leadership training to the teachers and principals of twenty-five of the first eighty-two schools that will be switching to the new school-based management system. Each of the twenty-five schools will be paired with an IBM executive who will donate about twenty days a year to the school. In addition, the executives will spend one weekend with their respective school committee at the IBM

THE ACADEMIES OF FINANCE

Eight years ago, American Express decided to do something about the fact that so many high school graduates seeking entry-level jobs at the company were deficient in basic mathematics, English, and work skills.

The company approached the New York City Board of Education in 1982 to develop a partnership program that would prepare high school students for jobs in the financial services industry. The result, the Academy of Finance, was not corporate checkbook philanthropy but an active working, long-term program with built-in accountability.

The components of the program include a special academy curriculum for juniors and seniors in high school, training programs for high school teachers, field trips, paid summer internships at sponsoring firms for students and teachers in the program, an advisory board in each city where there is an academy program, and an academy manager in each city.

The first Academy of Finance was launched at John Dewey High School in Brooklyn, New York, in 1982 with 35 students. By the 1990-91 school year, more than 2,400 students were enrolled in forty-five academy programs in seventeen cities nationwide. Of these, 62 percent are inner-city minority youngsters, 58 percent are women, and approximately 90 percent pursue college degrees after graduating.

The success of the Academy of Finance led American Express to launch the Academy of Travel and Tourism in 1984 and the National Academy Foundation (NAF) in 1989. An independent organization, NAF is rapidly expanding the number of academies around the nation. It also promotes the academy concept to other business sectors throughout the country. In 1990, the Ford Academy of Manufacturing Sciences and the Academy of Public Service in Washington, D.C., were launched. Besides American Express, more than 200 companies sponsor NAF, including Primerica, Ford, Peat Marwick, and the American Stock Exchange.

SOURCE: American Express.

facility in Palisades, New York. Other companies participating in the New York City training project are Coopers & Lybrand, New York Telephone, and NatWest Bank, U.S.A.

Companies should also explore the feasibility of working with child care providers and the operators of preschool programs in this way to offer them the managerial expertise few currently have.

9. Integrate related efforts. Business can help states create a better integration of policies and programs that address the development and education of children and the strengthening of the family unit. Policies and programs in these areas are seldom under the jurisdiction of a single government department or legislative committee. Administratively, most states divide the responsibility in this area among multiple departments, including education, labor, human resources, and health. Legislative committees overseeing these same areas are similarly divided. A number of states, including Connecticut, have established children's commissions to explore ways to improve the delivery of services to children and families.

10. Monitor and assess results. Measures of performance are essential to monitoring and assessing the results and progress of reform efforts. However, it is also important to establish a means of measuring results at the start of reform efforts as a way of identifying specific outcomes whose accomplishment can be objectively assessed. Goals should be established first, and measures should be found to match them, rather than the other way around.

Current measures of student performance are notoriously poor at evaluating such desirable results of student achievement as critical-thinking skills. Likewise, there are no precise ways to measure the results of early childhood education programs or child care except to track the progress of children through school to gauge how well they are performing academically and socially.

*   *   *

The future of America depends on the abilities of its people. Business has an abiding interest and a critical stake in ensuring that today's children grow up to be tomorrow's literate, skilled, adaptable adults who can work more effectively and productively. In view of its special interest, it is incumbent upon business to take the lead in pressing for needed change in policies and practices that affect child development and education, to lend its expertise to help create and sustain the restructuring of these systems, and to become the key advocate of children in the public policy process.

ENDNOTES

CHAPTER 1

1. Gary Natriello, Edward L. McDill, Aaron M. Pallas, *Schooling Disadvantaged Children: Racing Against Catastrophe*, Teachers College Press, New York, 1990, pp. 30-31.

2. Committee for Economic Development, *An America That Works: The Life-Cycle Approach to a Competitive Work Force*, 1990.

3. P. Michael Timpane and Laurie Miller McNeill, *Business Impact on Education and Child Development Reform*, Committee for Economic Development, 1991.

4. John Chubb and Terry Moe, *Politics, Markets, & America's Schools*, Brookings Institution, 1990.

5. Harold L. Hodgkinson, *The Same Client: The Demographics of Education and Service Delivery Systems*, Institute for Educational Leadership, Inc./Center for Demographic Policy, 1989, page 3.

6. The National Commission to Prevent Infant Mortality, *Troubling Trends: The Health of America's Next Generation*, Washington, D.C., February 1990.

7. *The Forgotten Half: Pathways to Success for America's Youth and Young Families*, Final Report of the William T. Grant Foundation Commission on Work, Family, and Citizenship, November 1988, page 21.

8. Hodgkinson, *The Same Client*.

9. U.S. House of Representatives, Select Committee on Children, Youth, and Families, Highlights of Program Effects, 1990.

CHAPTER 2

1. Lisbeth B. Schorr and Daniel Schorr, *Within Our Reach: Breaking the Cycle of Disadvantage*, Anchor Press, Doubleday, New York, 1988.

2. Schorr and Schorr, *Within Our Reach*.

3. Deborah L. Cohen, "Joining Forces," *Education Week*, March 15, 1989.

4. Ellen Galinsky and Dana Friedman, "Education Before School: Investing in Quality Child Care," unpublished research paper prepared for CED project on Child Care, 1990.

5. Dana Friedman, Families and Work Institute, *NY Times*, March 15, 1990.

6. The National Head Start Association, *Head Start: The Nation's Pride, A Nation's Challenge*, Report of the Silver Ribbon Panel, May 1990.

7. Dominic F. Gullo, "The Effects of Gender, At Risk Status, and Number of Years in Preschool on Children's Academic Readiness," University of Wisconsin-Milwaukee, Department of Early Childhood Education, 1990.

CHAPTER 3

1. "Contentions Regarding Public Education," a report of the Education Task Force of the Minnesota Business Partnership, September 28, 1990.

2. Paul T. Hill, Arthur E. Wise, and Leslie Shapiro, *Educational Progress: Cities Mobilize to Improve Their Schools*, Rand Center for the Study of the Teaching Profession, January 1989.

3. John Witte, "Understanding High School Achievement: After a Decade of Research, Do We Have Any Confident Policy Recommendations?," prepared for delivery at the 1990 Annual Meeting of the American Political Science Association, August 30 - September 2, 1990.

4. Committee for Economic Development, *Investing in Our Children: Business and the Public Schools*, 1985, pp. 28-29.

5. U.S. General Accounting Office, "Many Proprietary Schools Do Not Comply With the Department of Education's Pell Grant Requirements," August 20, 1984.

6. National Commission on Testing and Public Policy, *From Gatekeeper to Gateway: Transforming Testing in America*, Boston College, Boston, Massachusetts, 1990.

7. Allen Odden, "State Policy for At-Risk Children: Preschool to High School," *Time for Results: Task Force on Readiness*, National Governors' Association Center for Policy Research and Analysis, 1986, p. 52., and *Business Week*, "The Money Questions that Have Schools Stumped," June 4, 1990, pp. 98-99.

8. CED, *Investing in Our Children*, p. 20.

9. William A. Firestone, Susan H. Fuhrman, and Michael W. Kirst, *The Progress of Reform, An Appraisal of State Education Initiatives*, Center for Policy Research in Education, Eagleton institute of Politics, Rutgers, The State University of New Jersey, New Brunswick, New Jersey, 1990, pg. 41.

10. *Newsweek*, "The New Teacher Corps," July 16, 1990.

CHAPTER 4

1. Timpane and Miller McNeill.

2. Timpane and Miller McNeill.

3. Timpane and Miller McNeill.

4. National Head Start Association, *Head Start: The Nation's Pride, A Nation's Challenge* and M. Therese Gnezda and Shelley L. Smith, *Child Care and Early Childhood Education Policy: A Legislator's Guide*, National Conference of State Legislatures, Washington, D.C., March 1989.

5. Timpane and Miller McNeill.

6. Firestone, et. al.

7. California Department of Education, *Opening Doors: California Education Reform*, Annual Report, 1989.

8. These Business Roundtable publications are *The Business Role in State Education Reform*, by R. Scott Fosler, Committee for Economic Development, 1990, and *The Business Roundtable Participation Guide: A Primer for Business on Education*, prepared by the National Alliance of Business, 1990.

9. This section is adapted from *The Business Role in State Education Reform*, by R. Scott Fosler, Committee for Economic Development, prepared for the Business Roundtable, 1990.

MEMORANDA OF COMMENT, RESERVATION, OR DISSENT

Page 4, GEORGE C. EADS

I believe that this paragraph unfairly characterizes the argument made by Chubb and Moe (the study cited) and, more importantly, downplays the importance of meaningful choice as an essential element in reforming education in this country. While Chubb and Moe may go too far in arguing that choice is a panacea for the country's educational needs, the present study errs in the opposite direction by overstating the impact that the various educational reforms it endorses can have without including as a central element in the nation's educational strategy some meaningful method of allowing parents to "vote with their feet."

Page 47, JAMES Q. RIORDAN, with which ELMER B. STAATS has asked to be associated.

I agree with the publication of the *The Unfinished Agenda: A New Vision for Child Development and Education* which states again the urgent need to provide *all* children with the early help needed to prepare them for school and to provide a good school system. The report emphasizes the desirability of involving parents in the process and urges flexibility and innovation in the education structure. I disagree, however, with the negative thrust of the section on choice. I agree that a successful public school system is a primary objective but it seems to me that the restriction of choice should not be necessary for that success.

Choice may well encourage the managers of the existing structure to redouble their efforts to make the improvements in the public school system (including choice within that system) that we recommend. In at least some cases choice may help generate parent and community participation that would not otherwise be forthcoming. An empowered parent may well become a more involved parent. Choice is not perfect – but the existing arrangements are not perfect. If choice does not help it will not be greatly used. If, however, it works it may well work twice – once in the choice schools themselves and again in the motivation it will generate in the management of the rest of the school system.

Page 47, HENRY SCHACHT

We would recommend dropping the word *public* in the title of this section and in the second paragraph because the word will confuse readers. As the section later clarifies, "public school choice" is a limited effort to give parents options among public schools. A pure choice program would allow parents to choose any school, whether historically public, private, or parochial, which best meets their children's needs.

Page 47, HENRY SCHACHT

The worst thing we could do is to leave matters as they are. As it is, many disadvantaged students are already confined to inferior schools because of geographic requirements. But choice, coupled with aggressive information, counseling, and outreach can give these children an opportunity – an opportunity they do not have now – to attend an accredited school that will provide them with the quality education that they need.

Page 49, GEORGE C. EADS

I disagree. I believe that choice systems should involve *all* schools, public and private, meeting certain well-defined criteria. To limit choice plans to the public schools would significantly undercut the effectiveness of choice as a tool for educational reform.

Page 49, HENRY SCHACHT

Limiting parental choice to historically public schools perpetuates the existing inequity: only those wealthy enough to move to another public school district or to pay private school tuition have real choice. The direct, immediate challenge of existing private schools and freely chartered new schools is needed to cause the degree and speed of change necessary to effect the improvement needed in public schools. State support which is directed by the parent to any accredited school should constitute "public support." Thus, all accredited schools become "public" schools.

Page 49, HENRY SCHACHT

Citing proprietary schools as an example of abuse in choice in higher education is truly stretching the point. Proprietary schools (which unlike any other part of our system of elementary, secondary and higher education are for profit) are largely vocational in nature and have never been considered to be part of our nation's "system" of higher education, which is considered unexcelled anywhere else in the world. If anything, using proprietary schools as an example of abuse only strengthens the case that choice has been the key ingredient in assuring quality in our nation's colleges and universities.

Page 53, DONALD M. STEWART

As an organization that uses multiple assessment methods – including essays, portfolios, and multiple choice tests – the College Board endorses the CED position that multiple assessment formats may well be essential to measuring what is achieved in our educational improvement efforts. As the discussion about providing appropriate assessment continues, two points need constant attention.

First, whatever methods are used, in order to have a comprehensive, accurate, and productive assessment effort it is most important to define and agree upon what we value as results. For if we do not, we will assuredly begin to value – in the sense of teaching – that which we assess.

Second, as the process of defining our educational goals and selecting appropriate assessment methods unfold, we must be willing to make tradeoffs among such factors as cost, objectivity, time requirements, and so on.

These issues will require constant vigilance as we all work to serve better the many needs and situations of new generations of students. The College Board stands ready to help in that enterprise.

We wish to give special thanks to the following foundations and companies whose generous support made this policy statement possible.

Aetna Foundation, Inc.

Carnegie Corporation of New York

The Clorox Company Foundation

Daiwa Securities Company Ltd. of Tokyo

Eastman Kodak Company

Exxon Education Foundation

The George Gund Foundation

GTE Foundation

The William and Flora Hewlett Foundation

The Kraft General Foods Foundation

Lilly Endowment, Inc.

Morgan Stanley Group, Inc.

Charles Stewart Mott Foundation

Northern Telecom

NYNEX Foundation

The Pew Charitable Trusts

Pittway Corporation Charitable Foundation

Primerica Foundation

The Rockefeller Foundation

OBJECTIVES OF THE COMMITTEE FOR ECONOMIC DEVELOPMENT

For over forty years, the Committee for Economic Development has been a respected influence on the formation of business and public policy. CED is devoted to these two objectives:

To develop, through objective research and informed discussion, findings and recommendations for private and public policy that will contribute to preserving and strengthening our free society, achieving steady economic growth at high employment and reasonably stable prices, increasing productivity and living standards, providing greater and more equal opportunity for every citizen, and improving the quality of life for all.

To bring about increasing understanding by present and future leaders in business, government, and education, and among concerned citizens, of the importance of these objectives and the ways in which they can be achieved.

CED's work is supported by private voluntary contributions from business and industry, foundations, and individuals. It is independent, non-profit, nonpartisan, and nonpolitical.

Through this business-academic partnership, CED endeavors to develop policy statements and other research materials that commend themselves as guides to public and business policy; that can be used as texts in college economics and political science courses and in management training courses; that will be considered and discussed by newspaper and magazine editors, columnists, and commentators; and that are distributed abroad to promote better understanding of the American economic system.

CED believes that by enabling business leaders to demonstrate constructively their concern for the general welfare, it is helping business to earn and maintain the national and community respect essential to the successful functioning of the free enterprise capitalist system.

STATEMENTS ON NATIONAL POLICY ISSUED BY THE COMMITTEE FOR ECONOMIC DEVELOPMENT

SELECTED PUBLICATIONS:

An America That Works: The Life-Cycle Approach to a Competitive Work Force *(1990)*

Breaking New Ground in U.S. Trade Policy *(1990)*

Battling America's Budget Deficits *(1989)*

*Strengthening U.S.-Japan Economic Relations *(1989)*

Who Should Be Liable? A Guide to Policy for Dealing with Risk *(1989)*

Investing in America's Future: Challenges and Opportunities for Public Sector Economic Policies *(1988)*

Children in Need: Investment Strategies for the Educationally Disadvantaged *(1987)*

Finance and Third World Economic Growth *(1987)*

Toll of the Twin Deficits *(1987)*

Reforming Health Care: A Market Prescription *(1987)*

Work and Change: Labor Market Adjustment Policies in a Competitive World *(1987)*

Leadership for Dynamic State Economies *(1986)*

Investing in our Children: Business and the Public Schools *(1985)*

Fighting Federal Deficits: The Time for Hard Choices *(1985)*

Strategy for U.S. Industrial Competitiveness *(1984)*

Strengthening the Federal Budget Process: A Requirement for Effective Fiscal Control *(1983)*

Productivity Policy: Key to the Nation's Economic Future *(1983)*

Energy Prices and Public Policy *(1982)*

Public-Private Partnership: An Opportunity for Urban Communities *(1982)*

Reforming Retirement Policies *(1981)*

Transnational Corporations and Developing Countries: New Policies for a Changing World Economy *(1981)*

Fighting Inflation and Rebuilding a Sound Economy *(1980)*

Stimulating Technological Progress *(1980)*

Helping Insure Our Energy Future: A Program for Developing Synthetic Fuel Plants Now *(1979)*

Redefining Government's Role in the Market System *(1979)*

Improving Management of the Public Work Force: The Challenge to State and Local Government *(1978)*

Jobs for the Hard-to-Employ: New Directions for a Public-Private Partnership *(1978)*

An Approach to Federal Urban Policy *(1977)*

Key Elements of a National Energy Strategy *(1977)*

Nuclear Energy and National Security *(1976)*

Fighting Inflation and Promoting Growth *(1976)*

Improving Productivity in State and Local Government *(1976)*

*International Economic Consequences of High-Priced Energy *(1975)*

Broadcasting and Cable Television: Policies for Diversity and Change *(1975)*

Achieving Energy Independence *(1974)*

A New U.S. Farm Policy for Changing World Food Needs *(1974)*

Congressional Decision Making for National Security *(1974)*

*Toward a New International Economic System: A Joint Japanese-American View *(1974)*

More Effective Programs for a Cleaner Environment *(1974)*

The Management and Financing of Colleges *(1973)*

Financing the Nation's Housing Needs *(1973)*

Building a National Health-Care System *(1973)*

High Employment Without Inflation: A Positive Program for Economic Stabilization *(1972)*

Reducing Crime and Assuring Justice *(1972)*

Military Manpower and National Security *(1972)*

The United States and the European Community: Policies for a Changing World Economy *(1971)*

Social Responsibilities of Business Corporations *(1971)*

Education for the Urban Poor: From Preschool to Employment *(1971)*

Further Weapons Against Inflation *(1970)*

Making Congress More Effective *(1970)*

Training and Jobs for the Urban Poor *(1970)*

Improving the Public Welfare System *(1970)*

* Statements issued in association with CED counterpart organizations in foreign countries.

CED COUNTERPART ORGANIZATIONS
IN FOREIGN COUNTRIES

Close relations exist between the Committee for Economic Development and independent, nonpolitical research organizations in other countries. Such counterpart groups are composed of business executives and scholars and have objectives similar to those of CED, which they pursue by similarly objective methods. CED cooperates with these organizations on research and study projects of common interest to the various countries concerned. This program has resulted in a number of joint policy statements involving such international matters as energy, East-West trade, assistance to developing countries, and the reduction of nontariff barriers to trade.

CE	Circulo de Empresarios Serano Jover 5-2º Madrid 8, Spain
CEDA	Committee for Economic Develoment of Australia 139 Macquarie Street, Sydney 2001 New South Wales, Australia
CEPES	Europaische Vereinigung für Wirtschafliche und Soziale Entwicklung Reuterweg 14, 6000 Frankfurt/Main, West Germany
IDEP	Institut de l'Enterprise 6, rue Clément-Marot, 75008 Paris, France
経済同友会	Keizai Doyukai (Japan Federation of Business Executives) Japan Industrial Club Building 1 Marunouchi, Chiyoda-ku, Tokyo, Japan
PSI	Policy Studies Institute 100, Park Village East, London NW1 3SR, England
SNS	Studieförbundet Näringsliv Samhälle Sköldungagatan 2, 11427 Stockholm, Sweden